Prais

Comple.

lead book in the Loving Jesus Without Limits series

"Soulful and engaging."
—PUBLISHER'S WEEKLY

"Shannon Ethridge's life exhibits God's transforming power. Her response to tragedy will guide others who struggle through dark valleys, to find the light of hope that is in Christ."
—MAX LUCADO, best-selling author

"When the worst has happened, only time can bring perspective and turn trauma into triumph. Shannon Ethridge is an incredible woman who has a story to tell and a passion to share. Through experiences that would level most, she has risen as a lover of Jesus who can speak to the heart of every woman. *Completely His* calls even the most timid or scarred to a place of deep, sweet relationship with the One who patiently waits for His beloved to lean in and trust Him. I loved the book. I love Shannon's heart."
—JAN SILVIOUS, author of *Foolproofing Your Life*
and *Big Girls Don't Whine*

"Insightful and daring, *Completely His* so challenged me to look at myself honestly and ask 'Am I *all* yours, God?' Shannon is completely vulnerable as she shares a longing for God in every area of her life and a step-by-step example of how to walk with Him in all aspects of daily living. This message is encouraging, life changing, and much needed by every one of us."
—SHAUNTI FELDHAHN, best-selling author of *For Women Only*
and *For Men Only*

Other books by Shannon Ethridge

Completely His
Completely Loved
Completely Forgiven
Every Woman's Battle
Every Woman's Battle Workbook
Every Young Woman's Battle
Every Young Woman's Battle Workbook
Every Single Woman's Battle
Every Woman, Every Day
Every Woman's Battle Promise Book
Preparing Your Daughter for Every Woman's Battle
Every Woman's Marriage
Every Woman's Marriage Workbook
Words of Wisdom for Women at the Well
Words of Wisdom for Well Women

LOVING JESUS
A 30-DAY GUIDE
WITHOUT LIMITS

COMPLETELY
Blessed

Discovering God's Extraordinary Gifts

SHANNON ETHRIDGE

Best-selling author of the Every Woman's Battle series

WATERBROOK
PRESS

COMPLETELY BLESSED
PUBLISHED BY WATERBROOK PRESS
12265 Oracle Boulevard, Suite 200
Colorado Springs, Colorado 80921
A division of Random House Inc.

Italics in Scripture quotations indicate the author's added emphasis.

Details in some anecdotes and stories have been changed to protect the identities of the
persons involved.

ISBN 978-1-4000-7114-2

Library of Congress Cataloging-in-Publication Data
Ethridge, Shannon.
    Completely blessed : discovering God's extraordinary gifts / Shannon Ethridge.—1st ed.
    p. cm.
Includes bibliographical references and indexes.
    ISBN 978-1-4000-7114-2
    1. Christian women—Prayers and devotions. 2. God—Love. I. Title.
    BV4844.E825 2007
    242'.643—dc22

                                        2007016327

Printed in the United States of America
2007—First Edition

10 9 8 7 6 5 4 3 2 1

SPECIAL SALES
Most WaterBrook Multnomah books are available in special quantity discounts when
purchased in bulk by corporations, organizations, and special interest groups. Custom
imprinting or excerpting can also be done to fit special needs. For information, please
e-mail SpecialMarkets@WaterBrookPress.com or call 1-800-603-7051.

Contents

AN INVITATION INTO THE GENEROSITY OF GOD

*W*hat did you get me?" That's the question my children always ask around their birthdays and Christmas. I hope they've learned that it's more blessed to give than to receive, but who doesn't love to get gifts? Especially really good ones!

Speaking of good gifts, look what God says about the gifts He gives to us.

> I love all who love me. Those who search for me will surely find me.
> Unending riches, honor, wealth, and justice are mine to distribute.
> My gifts are better than the purest gold, my wages better than sterling silver! I walk in righteousness, in paths of justice. Those who
> love me inherit wealth, for I fill their treasuries. (Proverbs 8:17–21)

Better than gold or silver? Riches, honor, and wealth *without end*? Treasuries *overflowing*? Wow! What a great gift giver God must be to grant His people such love, favor, and blessing. Fortunately, He doesn't make us wait until our birthdays or Christmas to open these extraordinary gifts. We can unwrap and enjoy them every day and even share them with others without worrying about blowing our gifts budget.

Welcome to *Completely Blessed*, the third devotional book in a series of four, which are intended to follow the lead book, *Completely His: Loving Jesus Without Limits*. If you've not yet read *Completely His* or the first two devotionals, I encourage you to do so to ensure you get the most from the series. But if you choose to read this book first, you'll still be enriched by it—and the three other devotionals in the series.

Each of the devotionals is designed to deepen your commitment to your heavenly Bridegroom, Jesus Christ, and to help you embrace your role as His beloved bride. In these thirty-day devotionals, we'll carefully consider the following:

- how far God has gone to reveal Himself to us and draw us closer (explored in *Completely Loved: Recognizing God's Passionate Pursuit of Us*)
- how God can use you mightily in spite of your shortcomings (demonstrated in *Completely Forgiven: Responding to God's Transforming Grace*)
- how God lavishes both His presence and His presents upon us (the message in this devotional)
- how our love for God cannot be contained but can be shared naturally (examined in *Completely Irresistible: Drawing Others to God's Extravagant Love*)

The first devotional focuses on God's interactions with various people in the Old Testament in order to gain a clearer glimpse into His character and to understand how He passionately pursues us. The second devotional takes a closer look at some of those saints and sinners in the Bible, as well as God's reaction to them, so that we can celebrate the forgiveness we've found in Christ. In this devotional, we'll unwrap some of the mysteries contained in the New Testament as to the wonderful blessings we've been given by our generous and thoughtful God. We'll consider such questions as:

- What are some of the unique gifts God grants to us that continually add to the quality of our existence?
- What blessings do we glean from applying Christ's ancient parables to our modern-day lives?
- What part does God invite us to play in His great salvation drama?
- How can I cultivate a heart overflowing with gratitude toward my generous God for the multitude of blessings He bestows upon me?

Over the next thirty days, we'll consider such things as lilies, light loads, and lead roles. We'll examine the value of compassionate friends, firm foundations, and fertile soil. We'll celebrate prodigal sons, prayer, green pastures, and the promise of paradise. We'll join Jesus at wedding banquets, watch Him turn water into wine, and even go walking on the water.

I'm so glad you'll be joining us on this thirty-day journey. Get ready to be showered with blessings as we consider many of the most extraordinary gifts one could ever hope to receive!

A GIFT THAT KEEPS ON GIVING

Daily reading: John 1:1–18

Key passage: In the beginning the Word already existed. He was with God, and he was God. He was in the beginning with God. He created everything there is. Nothing exists that he didn't make. Life itself was in him, and this life gives light to everyone…. The one who is the true light, who gives light to everyone, was going to come into the world….

We have all benefited from the rich blessings he brought to us—one gracious blessing after another. (John 1:1–4, 9, 16)

*W*ANTED: SAVIOR OF THE WORLD
Applicant must…
- be able to transcend space and time,
- intimately know God and represent Him perfectly,
- be willing to leave paradise and live as a homeless person,
- dwell among people who doubt your credentials and question your sanity,
- be willing to tirelessly heal the sick, encourage the poor, and love the unlovely,

- serve as a light in a dark world and overcome all forms of evil, and
- single-handedly bear the weight of the world's iniquities.

Only the sinless need apply. Send résumé directly to God.

If you are thinking that no one could have filled God's job description for a savior besides Jesus, you are absolutely right. Even before humankind fell into sin, God had a perfect plan to restore us into right relationship and sweet fellowship with Him. His restoration plan didn't come in the form of a prescription or an extreme makeover. It came in the form of a person—a timeless, sinless, and matchless person by the name of Jesus Christ.

Admittedly, the gospel of John's opening lines can be confusing for the person who doesn't recognize the incredible credentials our Savior holds. I recall as a teenager hearing my pastor read the following: "In the beginning was the Word, and the Word was with God, and the Word was God" (John 1:1, NIV). The verse sounded to me like an unsolvable riddle. But now I know that Jesus (the Word) was God made flesh, sent to earth to dwell among us.

Jesus' origins go back much further than Mary's womb. He existed with God before the beginning of time and will continue to exist when time has ended. But Jesus hadn't just been *with* God, like two people can be with each other in a room. As part of the Trinity—God the Father, Jesus the Son, and the Holy Spirit—He actually *is* God.

In other words, God Himself came to the earth He created. Why? To demonstrate His lavish love. He desired to be with us for a time and to leave an indelible mark on the history of humanity—indeed, to save us from ourselves and our folly. God came down from heaven in the form of a human being so that we could recognize and relate with Him in an intimate way and learn from Him how we are to live. Can you imagine a more extraordinary and personal gift?

God's gifts to us are as timeless as He is. Just because we're living two thousand years after Jesus walked this earth doesn't mean we have missed out on having a personal relationship with Him. Does Jesus still transcend time and space? You bet. He is both omniscient (knowing all things throughout time) and omnipresent (everywhere at once). Not only that, the gospel accounts of His life teach us how to intimately know Him. Can Jesus still heal the sick, encourage the poor, and love the unlovely? Yes, He can, and He does so countless times per day. Is He still our light in a dark world? Does He overcome evil still to this day? Does He gladly bear the weight of every sin we commit? Yes, yes, and yes.

God didn't just send a postcard from heaven or a mere memento or token of His love. He gave us a precious gift that keeps on giving. He gave us a living, breathing, walking, talking, loving, healing, teaching, preaching example of His extraordinary love by coming near to us in the form of His Son, Jesus Christ.

HOLDING HIS HAND

Name three reasons why God sent Himself to this earth.

_____

_____

_____

_____

Could God have sent us a greater gift? Why or why not?

_____

_____

_____

_____

How does God's gift to us, the gift of Jesus Christ as our Savior, continue to keep giving and giving? What blessings do we continue to receive through Christ's life, death, and resurrection?

_____

_____

_____

_____

Heavenly Father,

It boggles our minds to try to think of a more perfect plan than the one You devised and executed. Thank You for coming near to us in the form of Your Son, Jesus, to bring light to our world, to save us from our sins, and to show us how to live in obedience and sweet fellowship with You. In Jesus' name. Amen.

AN UNDENIABLE SIGN

Daily reading: Isaiah 42:1; Matthew 3:13–17; Luke 4:14–22; John 1:29–34

Key passage: John said, "I saw the Holy Spirit descending like a dove from heaven and resting upon him. I didn't know he was the one, but when God sent me to baptize with water, he told me, 'When you see the Holy Spirit descending and resting upon someone, he is the one you are looking for. He is the one who baptizes with the Holy Spirit.' I saw this happen to Jesus, so I testify that he is the Son of God." (John 1:32–34)

We had just put the groceries away on August 16, 1977, when my mother announced that she was lying down for a nap. Promising not to disturb her, I turned the television volume down low and sprawled out near the set on the green shag carpet. Mom had probably just dozed off when I heard the television announcer make a shocking statement. I went running into her bedroom screaming and crying, "Mom, guess who died!"

She sat straight up in bed, looking terrified, and asked, "Who?"

"ELVIS!" I replied, expecting her to share my heartbreak. Instead, she was furious that I panicked her in such a way.

Knowing I was a big Elvis fan, my mom surprised me three years later. We were on our way back to Texas from Alabama when we stopped in Memphis,

Tennessee. She thought I would enjoy seeing Elvis's palatial home, Graceland, and indeed I did. At that time there was no one greater in my eyes. While standing in line outside the surrounding fence, I overheard one woman talking about how she went to elementary school with Elvis in Tupelo, Mississippi. I can still hear her screechy southern voice declare in astonishment, "Why, he was no big deal back then—just a regular little kid! We had no idea he'd become the King of Rock 'n' Roll!"

As I read today's passage of Scripture, I couldn't help but wonder if John the Baptist and others around Nazareth were thinking something similar about Jesus. *Why, He's just Joseph and Mary's kid! We've known Him all our lives! He couldn't possibly be God's anointed Messiah, could He? King of kings? Lord of lords? Surely not.*

Jesus' humble beginnings did not match the Jews' expectations for the Messiah. As they awaited His arrival, they were looking toward the mansions, not the mangers…scouting for a prince, not a pauper…watching for a warrior on a gallant white steed, not a meek man on a lowly donkey. Boy, were they wrong.

Perhaps this was one reason why God drew Jesus toward the waters of the Jordan River to be baptized by John. Jesus certainly didn't need to be baptized—the act symbolizes repentance from sin, of which Jesus had none. That's why I believe God had something else in mind. I think God wanted to give the people a clear, undeniable sign that Jesus was the One sent from heaven to demonstrate God's love and compassion.

Before God gave the sign, only John the Baptist had the spiritual eyes to recognize Jesus as God's own. As Jesus approached him, John declared, "Look! There is the Lamb of God who takes away the sin of the world! He is the one I was talking about when I said, 'Soon a man is coming who is far greater than I am, for he existed long before I did'" (John 1:29–30). But his very next words tell us that this was a brand-new revelation for him, as he says twice, in verses 31 and 33, "I *didn't know* he was the one." In other words, "I had no idea the one I've been preparing the way for is our very own Jesus!"

John the Baptist and Jesus were family, as their mothers were related to one another (Luke 1:36). In the first chapter of Luke's gospel, Mary, pregnant with Jesus, makes a lengthy trip from Nazareth to Judea to visit Elizabeth, who is pregnant with John. Mary stays with Elizabeth three months (Luke 1:56). Although we've no way of knowing for sure, I think it's safe to speculate that Jesus and John the Baptist knew each other as they were growing up, yet John had no idea that Jesus was the Messiah until that moment at the Jordan River. He must have been scratching his head in confusion, wondering, *This is the Son of God? Jesus? Our Jesus?*

Ready to begin His ministry on earth, Jesus enters the Jordan River and insists that John baptize Him. In these moments, the sky opens up and the Spirit of God visibly descends upon Jesus. God audibly speaks to John and all who were gathered there, saying, "This is my beloved Son, and I am fully pleased with him" (Matthew 3:17). Talk about an undeniable sign! There could no longer be any doubt in people's minds. They heard God with their own ears. They saw the dove descend with their own eyes. They knew the truth in their hearts—Jesus, *their Jesus*, was indeed the Messiah. God Himself had declared that Jesus was His Son.

Not only was this an undeniable sign to the Jews, it is a sign to us as well. God knows our tendency to question and doubt, and so He gave us this gift so that we would know that the King of the universe came to earth as one of us. He aligned Himself with us—hopeless sinners—in order that we could be made saints. He entered this world and served us in humility, then returned to heaven to be with the Father, giving us a foretaste of what is to come for us as well.

HOLDING HIS HAND

What do Jesus' humble beginnings say about our Savior?

_____

_____

_____

How does it make me feel to know that Jesus was willing to identify Himself with me, even though He was sinless? Why?

_____

_____

_____

What might be an appropriate expression of gratitude for how Christ humbled Himself and became one of us in order that He might love us, serve us, and save us?

_____

_____

_____

Lord Jesus,

Thank You for submitting to Your Father's plan for Your life, for truly I am the direct beneficiary of Your extravagant sacrifice. Although sinless, You took on my sins and identified Yourself with me completely. Now I declare, in response, that I am completely Yours. Amen.

POWER OVER THE ENEMY

Daily reading: Matthew 4:1–11; Luke 4:1–13

Key passage: Jesus said to him, "Away from me, Satan!…It is written…"
Then the devil left him. (Matthew 4:10–11, NIV)

*O*nce Jesus was filled with the Holy Spirit through baptism, the Spirit led Him into the desert to be tempted by Satan (Matthew 4:1). What transpires would make a great scene in an old Western movie. Use your imagination, read the following script with a Texas drawl, and see if you don't agree:

Jesus (wearing a white cowboy hat) goes without grub for forty days and nights. The devil (wearing a black cowboy hat) is licking his chops over the idea that Jesus is famished and vulnerable. However, Satan fails to realize that Jesus' spirit is strongest when his flesh is the weakest.

Satan invites Jesus to the Not-O-Kay Corral, trying to entice Him with food like a farmer dangles a carrot in front of a mule. "If You're the Son o' God, tell them there rocks to become bread, Jesus!" (Matthew 4:3).

"Why you yellow-bellied sapsucker, I ain't about to do no such thing! It says in My Father's book that man don't live on bread alone," Jesus replies. "I live by every word that flows out of My Daddy's mouth!" (verse 4).

Satan is thinking, *But You ain't et for forty days! Ain't You starving to death yet?* Jesus, on the other hand, is thinking, *I may be hungry, but I ain't stupid! My Daddy's gonna' feed Me, yessiree.*

Satan slips another shell into his shotgun, saying, "Why don't You prove Yourself, Cowboy! Throw Yourself off this here temple to prove to everybody that God's angels are gonna gallop up and rescue You."

Jesus doesn't even shake in His boots but boldly sticks His index finger into the barrel of Satan's gun. "It is written: don't test God. I ain't a-gonna play that game, Satan!" (verse 7).

In a desperate, final attempt to cause Jesus to stumble and fall into sin, the devil takes Him to a high mountain and says, "I'll give You this here mountain range and every other one like it, along with every flea-bitten town on the planet. All You gotta do, Jesus, is drop to Yer knees and worship me" (verses 8–9).

Jesus moseys over to Satan, looks at him with disgust in His eyes, and says, "Get outta' here, you lyin' coward! I ain't about to worship you or anybody else—just My Daddy!" (verse 10).

Satan slithers away with his fist in the air, yelling, "I'll be back! Just you wait!"

Jesus just smiles and replies, "Oh, I'll be on the lookout. You can bet yer bottom dollar!"

Okay, so the western touch may seem like a stretch, but you get the idea. Jesus sent Satan packing out of that desert with his tail between his legs. As a result, Jesus accomplished three things:

1. *He revealed His true character.* In spite of His hunger and weakness, He proved that He wasn't looking for any shortcuts to the fulfillment of God's plan for the salvation of humanity. He never backed away from doing what His Father asked Him to do.

2. *He revealed the nature of temptation versus sin.* Jesus demonstrated that experiencing temptation is not a sin and that temptation doesn't become sin without our permission.

3. *He revealed Satan's limitations.* Jesus proved that we have the power to resist Satan when we exercise the authority given to us in God's Word. When we do so, Satan will flee from us (James 4:7).

Perhaps you are thinking that God gave this authority only to Jesus. Not so. In Luke 10:19, Jesus tells us, "Look, I have given you authority over all the power of the enemy, and you can walk among snakes and scorpions and crush them. Nothing will injure you." In other words, we have the same power over Satan as Jesus had. What a tremendous gift!

Even though God grants us power over the enemy, the e-mails I receive every week in response to the Every Woman's Battle series tell me we've not unwrapped this precious gift. Women frequently say things such as, "I'm *stuck* in this extramarital affair," "I feel *powerless* over temptation," and "I have *no control* over my feelings any more." It's as if Satan has their hands and ankles tied with rope and is aiming a shotgun in their faces. I know that the desperation and weakness people feel is real, but I long to scream through cyberspace, "Satan's faking you out! His power over you isn't real! You're giving in to his torture when you have the strength to get up, get in his face, and command that he flee!"

Of course, in order to exercise our power to do that, we have to use the same weapon Jesus used. When we use the Word of God as a weapon against Satan, we are wielding the mighty sword of the Holy Spirit (Ephesians 6:17). Each of the three times He was tempted, Jesus wielded that sword in Satan's face, replying, "It is written...!"

Do you know what is written in God's Word concerning gunfights at the Not-O-Kay Corral? God predetermines the winner—the good guy. Light triumphs over darkness (John 1:5). God sends Satan fleeing every time when we call on His name in faith and obey His instructions on how to get ourselves out of such gunfights with the devil. So, use God's Word with full confidence, my dear sister, that He will give you power over the Enemy just as He promises. Then use that power for your benefit and for God's glory.

HOLDING HIS HAND

When I sense Satan challenging me to a gunfight at the Not-O-Kay Corral, do I panic in fear or stand in faith? Why?

_____

_____

_____

What areas of weakness does Satan like to attack in my life? What are three or four passages of Scripture that I could use as weapons when Satan tempts me in these areas?

_____

_____

_____

What difference would it make in my life if I unwrapped God's gift of power over the Enemy and utilized it every day?

_____

_____

_____

Dear Lord,

We're so grateful that You showed us how to have faith in Your Father's words, even in the face of temptation. Remind us that You have gift-wrapped this same power especially for us, and be with us as we confidently exercise our God-given authority over the Enemy. Amen.

BLESSINGS FOR BROKENNESS

Daily reading: Isaiah 61:1–3; Matthew 5:1–12

Key passage: Blessed are the poor in spirit, for theirs is the kingdom of heaven. (Matthew 5:3, NIV)

*I*t was a Thursday afternoon, and I was staring at a blank page on my laptop. I wanted to write about the Beatitudes, but I just didn't know what to say about them. I was struggling to understand the meaning of this famous sermon that Jesus preached. The Beatitudes don't extol character traits I long to have. Who clamors to be "poor in spirit" or "to mourn"? Why did Jesus say we must have these qualities—among others—if we want to be blessed? Obviously, I was failing to comprehend the meaning behind the words Jesus preached. I was also distracted by preparations for the women's retreat I was speaking at that weekend, so I turned my computer off and prayed, *Lord, You're going to have to give me a personal tutorial if You want me to write on the Beatitudes!*

The following Sunday, having returned from my retreat, I was sitting in church when our pastor asked us to turn to the fifth chapter of Matthew. My heart leaped when I realized I was about to get that tutorial through the words of a man with a passion and training for unraveling the mysteries of Scripture. My pastor posed the same question I had, "Why must we be poor in spirit and mournful in order to be blessed?" Had he been a fly on the wall of my office that Thursday when I was wrestling with this exact question? As he spoke, I realized that while I was examining this passage from the perspective of how we relate to life in general, Jesus was preaching from a different perspective—*how we relate to our own sin.* When we look at the passage through this lens, the Beatitudes make perfect sense.

What does "poor in spirit" mean? It means that our shortcomings produce in us a sense of spiritual bankruptcy. When we acknowledge that we have no righteousness of our own with which we can claim a place in heaven, then we are poised to receive the righteousness that only God can give.

What does it mean to "mourn"? Jesus isn't referring to the mourning we engage in when we lose a loved one, but rather, the mourning we should engage in at the realization of our sinful behavior and choices. When we mourn over the darkness that dwells in our own hearts, the Lord comforts us with assurance that His light is sufficient to overcome our darkness.

And why should we "hunger and thirst" for righteousness? Because such a stance acknowledges that God has something that we simply do not. When we are full of ourselves and our own self-righteousness (which is a complete farce), then there is no room to receive anything from God. Only when we present our emptiness to God are we in a position for Him to fill us. Indeed, when we experience brokenness over our own sin, we delight in the delivering power of our Lord.

I left the church encouraged that God had graciously given me the perspective I needed. However, God wasn't finished teaching me about the importance of our brokenness over sin. He was about to bring the message of the Beatitudes much closer to home for me through my daughter.

When I left for my retreat that Thursday afternoon prior, I gave clear instructions to fourteen-year-old Erin that until she finished a big school project that was due on Monday, she was not allowed to go anywhere or have any friends over. But when I returned home Saturday night, she had sweet-talked her dad into letting her have a friend spend the night, assuring him that she was "almost done" with her project and that she and her friend would work on it together. However, the project completely slipped her mind. Come Sunday evening, the night before the project was due, Erin still had several hours of work to do on it. Grace came in the form of assistance from her brother, father, and me. However, justice came in the form of a three-day grounding.

Over the next twenty-four hours, Erin received a series of lectures about the importance of priorities, honesty, obedience, and time management, just to name a few topics covered in our "sanctification sessions." Exasperated, she preferred that we just drop the subject. She was willing to accept her punishment and even wrote a sweet note about how she didn't want us to stay upset with her over the matter. However, something wasn't feeling right. Erin seemed to be regretful over the matter but not repentant. Rather than acknowledging her sin, she kept making excuses, such as, "I just wasn't thinking… I thought I was almost done with the project… I forgot that you said no friends over until I was finished." I had a hard time buying these lines from such a bright and conscientious student.

Monday evening we sat down and talked about the situation yet another time. I explained, "Erin, until you recognize what was operating in your heart when you made this series of poor choices, the likelihood of your repeating history is very great. Remember, God could see what you were thinking, and you need to recognize it too." We sent her inside to do the dinner dishes, and while standing at the kitchen sink, she must have allowed the Lord to soften her heart. She returned with a completely different attitude and tearfully explained, "I've been thinking about it, and I realize that I kept ignoring the voice inside my head telling me to work on the project. It was wrong of me, and I hope you'll forgive me."

Aha! The breakthrough I'd been waiting for! Of course, her father and I immediately assured our daughter that all was forgiven, and she collapsed in my arms, asking, "So you still love me?" If you are a parent, you know what a ridiculous question that is. Our kids could never do anything bad enough to make us stop loving them. As a result of Erin's brokenness and true repentance, she was able to receive the blessings of a clean conscience, forgiveness, and assurance that all is well. Her countenance lifted and her joy returned.

Guess what, girlfriend? That's a blessing God wants to give us as well. He wants to reward us when we are broken over our own sin. Once we acknowledge our need for repentance, God jumps for joy and shouts, *Hallelujah! The breakthrough I've been waiting for! Yes, I still love you, and I always will! Now lift your head high and rest assured that all is well.*

HOLDING HIS HAND

When I am entrenched in sin, do I make excuses for it? If so, what are those excuses I try to lean on?

_____

_____

_____

As I try to maintain my own self-righteousness, am I in a position to receive the righteousness that God longs to give me as a free gift? Why or why not?

_____

_____

_____

According to the Beatitudes, if I acknowledge my spiritual bankruptcy and mourn my own sin, how will God respond? Do I believe that my repentance will lead to eternal blessings? Why or why not?

_____

_____

_____

Heavenly Father,

Just as a parent wants a child to grow and learn from her mistakes, You long for us to humbly do the same. Forgive us when we fail to acknowledge our own sin, and help us cultivate repentant hearts. Make us keenly aware of both our spiritual bankruptcy and Your generous gifts of complete restoration and unconditional love. Amen.

A VITAL ROLE IN HIS PLAY

Daily reading: Matthew 5:13–16; Mark 4:21; 9:50
Key passage: You are the salt of the earth.... You are the light of the world. (Matthew 5:13–14)

---

*I*n junior high, I was quite the drama queen. I'm not referring to the typical "she turns a molehill into a mountain" type of drama queen (although I probably did that as well). I was one of the top actresses in the drama department, and I prided myself on always landing one of the coveted lead roles. To me, there was no thrill in playing a smaller part. I wanted lots of lines to memorize, lots of time front-and-center stage. I knocked myself out in every play, not just because I loved acting, but also because I loved my teacher, Mrs. Taylor. I wanted to represent her well to the audience, to let people know what a wonderful instructor she was.

As you reflect on the passages of Scripture that you read today, imagine Jesus as a drama coach. He's using the word pictures of salt and light to explain the vital role He has cast you to play in the drama of humanity.

How vital is salt? I accidentally found out while making homemade ice cream as a newlywed. I followed the recipe's directions verbatim. I carefully measured out every ounce of milk, heavy cream, and vanilla extract required, followed by the exact number of eggs and cups of sugar. I set the metal container into the wooden bucket, filled the surrounding gaps with ice, and plugged in the motor.

A short while later, I noticed most of the ice had melted, so I added more ice…and more…and more. The motor continued to run and run, never slowing down or signaling an end to the process. Once I exhausted my ice supply, I stopped the motor and removed the lid in anticipation of the creamy, frozen concoction. However, the mixture was still so thin I could have sipped it through a straw. I was unaware of the most vital ingredient in making homemade ice cream—rock salt. It lowers the temperature of the ice enough to freeze a container of homemade ice cream. Salt is a vital ingredient in many other recipes and has been used since ancient times as a preservative. Many foods would spoil before we ate them if it weren't for their salt content.

And how vital is light? Think back to the last power outage you experienced and what an inconvenience it was to have to stumble around in the dark. Once the electricity went off, what was the first thing you reached for? A flashlight or candle, both sources of light. We need light to function without tripping over the furniture or stubbing our big toes. Even so, we could probably learn to survive without artificial light if necessary. However, natural light is another story. Human beings absolutely cannot live without the sun's light. Every wheat field, vegetable garden, and fruit tree completely depends upon the sun's light rays in order to produce life-sustaining food. Light also enhances the quality of our health and moods, keeping our body's internal "circadian" clock in sync so that we are alert during the day and ready to sleep at night.[1]

Salt and light are huge blessings from our Creator God, and He has given us the charge and the opportunity to be similar blessings in other people's lives as well. He has given us a vital role that only Christians can play. We are to season the world with God's love, joy, peace, patience, kindness, goodness, faithfulness, gentleness, and self-control (Galatians 5:22–23). We are also to shed life-giving light in a dark and lonely world, promoting purity in an impure society, promoting truth to expose lies, and promoting knowledge that will dispel ignorance.

In short, God has blessed us by granting us the privilege of representing Jesus and continuing the work He started two thousand years ago. Through the passion and purity that drive our lives, we are to show the world what Jesus would do in every situation, giving others an opportunity to see what a wonderful teacher and savior He is. Jim Caviezel, the actor who played the part of Jesus in Mel Gibson's *The Passion of the Christ*, said in an interview that it was difficult to put into words what an honor it was to play that role. Granted, a great honor for him, but you and I have the honor of playing this role every single day, not just for a movie, but in real life. This is an enormous responsibility. We've not been given a once-in-a-lifetime role that ends after a short run. We've been given a lifetime role that has eternal ramifications. So let's rehearse our parts carefully and play them well, shall we?

HOLDING HIS HAND

Why does God bless me with opportunities to represent Him in this world?

_____

_____

_____

What did Jesus mean in Mark 9:50 when He encouraged His disciples not to lose their saltiness?

_____

_____

_____

How have I maintained my "saltiness" as a Christian?

_____

_____

_____

What are some ways that I can bring "light" to my world?

_____

_____

_____

> *Dearest Lord,*
>
> *We're amazed that You allow us not only to partner with You in Your work, but that You also give us such a vital role as history's drama continues to unfold. Help us to rehearse our lines carefully by studying Your Word and to perform with excellence by the power of Your Holy Spirit. Amen.*

AN INVITATION TO WALK ON WATER

Daily reading: Matthew 14:22–33; Mark 6:45–51; John 6:16–21

Key passage: Peter called to him, "Lord, if it's really you, tell me to come to you by walking on water."

"All right, come," Jesus said.

So Peter went over the side of the boat and walked on the water toward Jesus. (Matthew 14:28–29)

---

*S*aturday afternoons were rather slow in the neighborhood I grew up in on the outskirts of Greenville, Texas. A few moms in their backyards hanging wet clothes on the line…dads pushing their mowers around the lawn…a handful of kids playing hopscotch or marbles in someone's driveway. Regardless of what was going on in the neighborhood on a Saturday afternoon, I could usually count on one thing—Davy Rogers passing by on his bicycle.

My house was out of Davy's way, so I knew he wasn't just passing by en route to somewhere else. Nor was he passing by just to get my attention and keep peddling. He wanted to extend an invitation, hoping I'd join him on a bike ride down to the crawdad hole, which I usually did with great delight.

When Jesus "was about to pass by" His disciples on the night of that great storm (Mark 6:48, NIV), He didn't intend to walk by and ignore their plight. Nor did He want to challenge them to a race or to show off, saying, "Hey, look at what I can do!" He was passing by because He wanted to extend an invitation to those who wanted to walk with Him. Were the disciples willing to look beyond the wind and waves to recognize that Jesus was beckoning them to abandon their fears and embrace faith? Could they leave the safety and comfort of their boat and venture out onto the water?

Perhaps you are wondering why the disciples would want to be out on the water when they had a perfectly good boat underneath them. The reason is because Jesus was out there, not in the boat. Yet sadly, only one disciple out of twelve was brave enough to step out in faith in order to be nearer to Jesus. The other eleven chose to be spectators.

But for Peter, what an unforgettable night that must have been! He sees Jesus doing something no one has ever done before, and he says, "I'm going for it! I'm going out there to be with Jesus." His focus is completely on the Savior, not the storm. He tosses one leg over the side of the boat, then the other, as his buddies watch with their mouths hanging open. "Surely he's not going to… oh my stars, he's doing it!… Unbelievable! He's not sinking—he's walking on water!" What an amazing gift! Can you imagine what that must have felt like? To do something only God can do?

I believe that Jesus wants to bless us in the same way. He wants us to surrender our fears to Him so that He can do things through us that we could not do without His supernatural power.

As with Peter, our faith is often strong enough to get us out of the boat. Yet our faith weakens the moment the waves rise. When the going gets tough, we are often tempted to run (or swim) back to safety. But through this remarkable story, Jesus is saying, "Stay focused on Me, and it doesn't matter how high the waves in your life get. I'll sustain you if you'll let Me."

Perhaps you find yourself faced with an invitation from God to join Him out on the open waves, yet your fears keep you from venturing outside your comfort zone. In his wonderfully inspiring book *If You Want to Walk on Water, You've Got to Get Out of the Boat,* John Ortberg claims:

> I believe there is something—Someone—inside us who tells us there is more to life than sitting in the boat. You were made for something more than merely avoiding failure. There is something inside you that wants to walk on the water—to leave the comfort of routine existence and abandon yourself to the high adventure of following God.
>
> So let me ask you a very important question. *What's your boat?*
>
> Your boat is whatever represents safety and security to you apart from God himself. Your boat is whatever you are tempted to put your trust in, especially when life gets a little stormy. Your boat is whatever keeps you so comfortable that you don't want to give it up even if it's keeping you from joining Jesus on the waves. Your boat is whatever pulls you away from the high adventure of extreme discipleship.[1]

What comfort zones do you need to confront during this season of your life? Are you placing your faith in fleeting things such as finances? friendships? external beauty? education? success? material possessions? Do you fear who you'd be without these identity crutches to lean on? If so, consider what your spiritual life will be like if you never abandon such boats. Would you rather have creature comforts or the comfort of walking intimately with the Creator Himself?

Regardless of what keeps you from stepping out of your comfort zone, Jesus is offering you the same gift He gave to Peter. He is offering you His supernatural power to accomplish amazing things. He's giving you an invitation to join Him wherever He leads you, so that the two of you can walk—both on land and on water—together.

HOLDING HIS HAND

What kind of "water walking" experience might God be calling me to in this season of my life?

_____

_____

_____

What is my boat? What is the comfort zone that causes me to hesitate embarking on an adventure of extreme discipleship?

_____

_____

_____

How can I focus on God rather than on the discomfort or fear that I feel? What effect will it have on my life to focus on God instead of on my fear?

_____

_____

_____

Father God,

So often we cling to things that provide a sense of comfort and security, yet these are false supports in our lives. Our real security comes from knowing that we are directly in the center of Your will, even if that means riding the waves of uncertainty. Thank You for promising to always be with us, no matter how strong the storms of life may become. Amen.

THE WAY HOME

Daily reading: John 14:1–11

Key passage: Jesus told [Thomas], "I am the way, the truth, and the life. No one can come to the Father except through me." (John 14:6)

---

*A*fter four days in the unfamiliar city of Bulawayo, Zimbabwe, I was beginning to recognize certain sights and gain a sense of direction. I had been traveling throughout the area, speaking at high schools. We were staying with the Cotton family on the outskirts of town near the bush, which is a large area of land inhabited by wild animals and few people.

By the fourth day of speaking, I had exercised my mouth far more than my body and was eager to get out and stretch my legs. It was about five o'clock in the afternoon, and I still had one hour of daylight, which was plenty of time for an energizing power walk. I headed south, making a mental note to pay attention to which roads I turned on so as not to get lost.

I was about forty-five minutes into my walk when I realized my sense of direction wasn't as keenly developed as I had thought. The roads weren't looking familiar anymore, and with only ten or fifteen minutes of daylight left, I tried not to panic. Many other people were also walking along these residential roads, mostly men walking home from work. I mustered the courage to ask someone, "Could you tell me how to get to Burnside Road?" As he gave directions, it sounded as if I'd wandered much farther away than I fathomed possible. But trusting the man's guidance more than my own instincts, I started down the road he recommended.

The sun was sinking quickly over the horizon, and the temperature was dropping just as quickly. I began to worry, *With no streetlights, how will I find my way home in the dark? Will I even recognize the driveway if I manage to find the right road? How cold will it get out here? Am I a walking target for a lion or wildebeest?* I couldn't believe I had gotten myself into this predicament! I had no clue how I could get myself home. With no daylight left, no sense of direction, and no cell phone, I fought back tears of panic. I prayed, *Lord, I don't know my way home, but You do. Won't You show me?*

Suddenly Mrs. Cotton drove past me in her Land Rover, stopping as she recognized me. My panic melted into peace as I ran toward her vehicle and hopped in. "What are you doing on *this* road?" she asked. I explained that I got lost looking for Burnside Road, to which she responded, "But we don't live on Burnside Road. We live on Circular Drive in the Burnside neighborhood!" No wonder I was lost! I didn't even realize where I had actually come from! God-bumps formed on my arms and the back of my neck when Mrs. Cotton continued, "And I never drive down this road! A moment ago, I was saying to myself, 'Why am I driving down this road?'"

I knew why she was driving down this road. God had sent her to save me from the lions, wildebeests, darkness, and cold.

Even though we didn't arrive at her house until several minutes later, I ceased worrying once I got into Mrs. Cotton's car, for I knew I was truly homeward bound once inside the homeowner's vehicle. I didn't have to worry about wandering around lost and alone anymore.

God has done the same thing for us in relationship to our eternal home. He knows that we have little realization of where we actually came from or how to get to heaven on our own. He sent Jesus to be our Savior and to show us the way home, not just *one* way to get home, but the *only* way. And Jesus doesn't just know the way; He *is* the way to our heavenly Father.

Once we've aligned ourselves with Jesus, we have no more need to panic. He said to His disciples, "Don't be troubled. You trust God, now trust in me"

(John 14:1). He says the same to us today. We're never lost when we are in the arms of Jesus. He'll remain by our side, and He'll deliver us safely back to His heavenly home, where we can bask in the presence of our loving Father for all eternity.

HOLDING HIS HAND

Have I ever felt spiritually lost or unsure of where I was going in life? If so, how did it feel?

_____

_____

_____

How does it make me feel to know that Jesus has found me and is never going to leave my side?

_____

_____

_____

Write a prayer of thanks to Jesus for showing you the way to your eternal home.

_____

_____

_____

Father God,

_How can we ever express our gratitude for Your sending
Your Son to show us the way to You? We would be forever
lost without such a road map, yet we are forever found
because of Your faithful love and protective provision. Help
us cling to Christ's side until we are ushered into our heavenly home. Amen._

A FIRM FOUNDATION

Daily reading: Luke 6:46–49; 1 Corinthians 3:10–11

Key passage: No one can lay any other foundation than the one we already have—Jesus Christ. (1 Corinthians 3:11)

*A*s my daughter left for kindergarten one day, she had tucked into her backpack every cookie sheet I owned. Her class was doing an art project, and Erin's job was to bring three cookie sheets. No big deal since I wasn't planning on baking cookies that day.

I did, however, bake a birthday cake that afternoon for my elderly grandfather. Once I took the 9 x 13 cake pan out of the oven, I would normally have flopped it over onto a cookie sheet, frosted it once it cooled, and carried it to the nursing home on the sheet. But without my cookie sheets, the best I could come up with was a foil-covered broiler rack to serve as a makeshift carrier. But then I discovered that I only had about four inches left on the roll of foil. I had no choice but to flop the cake onto the broiler rack without a foil lining. I knew Sparky (my granddad) wouldn't care about the presentation as much as my presence.

By the time I brought the frosted cake to the nursing home, however, it looked like a Wavy Lay's potato chip or a piece of corrugated metal. It had sunk through the ridges of the broiler rack, creating a slightly rippled effect on top. Sparky got a kick out of his wavy cake, saying it reminded him of one of my grandmother's culinary masterpieces.

I remembered this story years later when we began building on to our existing log cabin, intending to double the size and transform it from a modest vacation house to a full-time homestead. The project was the equivalent of building a whole new house adjoining the one we were living in. We interviewed three potential contractors and solicited bids from each one. Every bid put us into shock, but we decided to go with the builder who seemed to have the best grasp of the scope of the project.

Before we began building, we were looking for places to cut costs. The bid included everything from cabinets and countertops to windows and wall texture. I envisioned all of these cosmetic components and didn't want to compromise one bit. I figured that we could cut costs on a less visible place, as I had noticed how much we were spending for things that we'd never see, such as insulation and electrical wiring. Then I realized that the figure estimated for the foundation was a huge chunk of change—in the neighborhood of fifteen percent of the total cost of the addition!

I inquired as to whether such an expensive foundation was overkill, but my husband assured me that if we were going to cut corners, the last place we should do it was the foundation. "It's not visible, but it's the most important part of the house, Shannon!" Immediately that birthday cake I had made for my grandfather came to mind. I realized that if I didn't put the house on a much firmer foundation than I had that cake, our home stood a good chance of sinking and rippling in a similar manner. So we cut a few cosmetic corners, and today we have a solid home that sits on a firm foundation.

Considering how important the foundation is to the strength of a structure, I'm not surprised that both Jesus and Paul used the analogy of a house's foundation to describe the role that Jesus plays in our lives. When we stand on Christ as our solid Rock, nothing can shake us. We can remain steadfast in the face of the fiercest of spiritual storms and emotional earthquakes. But those who do not have this strong spiritual foundation might fall apart when they are hit by life's challenges.

I frequently saw this in the funeral home where I worked as a young adult. Those who lacked faith, as evidenced in the funeral service they planned (wanting to avoid hymns and prayers to a God they doubted existed), often had a painful response to their loss. They grieved violently, as if they would never see their loved one again. However, those families who had faith in God had a supernatural sense of peace in the midst of their grief. They knew their loved one was in heaven, awaiting their reunion. The bumper sticker slogan is true: *Know Jesus, Know Peace. No Jesus, No Peace.*

The incredibly firm foundation that Jesus Christ offers us isn't outrageously expensive. In fact, it's a free gift. Of course, it wasn't free to Him, since He paid for it with His precious blood. But it's free to us for the asking.

HOLDING HIS HAND

What ripple effects do I see in other people's lives when they choose to build on a foundation other than Jesus Christ?

_____

_____

_____

In what ways has Jesus been a "firm foundation" in my life? How has He helped me withstand the storms of life?

_____

_____

_____

Although the gift of a firm foundation in Christ Jesus is a free gift, what value does it add to my life?

_____

_____

_____

Almighty God,

You are the Master Builder who gave us Jesus as a firm foundation upon which to build our lives. Thank You for the confidence that such a foundation brings. Please remind us that no storm can overcome us when we are so strongly supported by You. Amen.

A RESTING PLACE
FOR OUR WORRIES

Daily reading: Matthew 6:25–34; Luke 12:22–32

Key passage: Look at the lilies and how they grow. They don't work or make their clothing, yet Solomon in all his glory was not dressed as beautifully as they are. And if God cares so wonderfully for flowers that are here today and gone tomorrow, won't he more surely care for you? (Luke 12:27–28)

---

*I*f you are like me, you delight in being surprised by a bouquet of flowers. My family has learned that flowers can say just about everything I'd ever want to hear them say—*I love you. Congratulations. Happy Valentine's Day. Happy Mother's Day. Happy Birthday. I'm sorry.* Although it's a special treat rather than a regular occurrence for me to have fresh-cut flowers in the house, the bouquet that inspired today's devotional arrived two days ago as an apology from my husband for a few poorly chosen words spoken. One sniff of the fragrant stargazer lilies and I immediately forgave all offenses!

Why are women so mesmerized by flowers? I remember picking handfuls of daisies, daffodils, and even dandelions as a little girl. My brother kept telling me that dandelions were actually weeds, not flowers, but I didn't care. They looked like flowers to me, so I tucked them into my ponytail holders to give my hair a touch of sunny color. As a teenager, my attentions turned to puffy white chrysanthemums. Come time for the homecoming football game, I couldn't have cared less about the game or the homecoming experience for the alumni. It was all about the mum corsage I got to wear proudly on my shoulder. Speaking of shoulders, if a Valentine's Day passed without at least one rose—or twelve!—the love of my life ran the risk of getting a cold shoulder.

I believe that God is just as mesmerized by flowers, if not more so. What a creative genius He is to have crafted thousands of varieties of people-pleasing, nose-tickling, smile-producing, eye-popping flowers! Who can inhale the sweet fragrance and look at the delicate folds and intricate detail of a rose in full bloom and not know that God is an amazing artist? Who can drive by a field of bluebonnets, Indian paintbrushes, sunflowers, or poppies and not realize that God has a marvelous eye for color and beauty?

Flowers—some lilies in a field—caught Jesus' eye one day as well. Taken by what He saw, He seized the opportunity to teach His disciples (and us) a valuable lesson. "Look at the lilies and how they grow. They don't work or make their clothing, yet Solomon in all his glory was not dressed as beautifully as they are. And if God cares so wonderfully for flowers that are here today and gone tomorrow, won't he more surely care for you?" (Luke 12:27–28). Indeed, God has a passion not only for poppies, periwinkles, and petunias but also for people. He cares for and tends to our needs because we are His own and He loves us deeply. *We* are the pinnacle of His creation and His primary concern.

While God may use many lovely flowers to express a variety of sentiments to us, Jesus calls our attention to lilies in order to point out to us that He has given His children a special gift: a resting place for life's worries. He says to us still, *You are my pride and joy, and I will faithfully provide for all your needs. If I feed, water, and clothe the flowers of the field, won't I do the same for My beloved bride? Focus on Me and My kingdom, and I'll take care of you and yours. Let Me be a resting place for your worries.*

Do you worry about everyday life so much that you forget about the importance of promoting God's kingdom? Do you frequently fret over how the bills will be paid, where the grocery money is going to come from, or what you are going to wear? What good does your worrying do? Does fretting put food in the refrigerator? No. Can we clothe ourselves with cares and concerns? No. God wants us to hang up our worries and cast our cares upon Him. Of course, we must be faithful in doing what we can do. We must put forth our best effort to make an honest living and spend our money wisely. But we must trust that God will bless our efforts.

The next time you pass through the floral section at the grocery store, stop and smell the roses and a few of the other flowers that catch your eye. Meditate for a moment about how Jesus has given you a resting place for your worries, and believe wholeheartedly that God will tend to your needs as carefully as He clothes the flowers of the field.

HOLDING HIS HAND

When I see the beauty of flowers or smell their sweet aroma, am I prompted to praise my Father in heaven for being such a masterful artist? What flowers in particular make me stand in awe of His creativity, and why?

_____

_____

_____

Do I worry about things over which I have no control? If so, what do I hope to accomplish by worrying?

_____

_____

_____

What if, instead of succumbing to worry and fear, I exercised faith in God's abundant ability to provide for the needs of His people? How would such faith impact my everyday living?

_____

_____

_____

Precious Jesus,

Thank You for calling our attention to the lilies of the field and for all the other flowers that You place in our paths for our delight and enjoyment. Most of all, Lord, thank You for what these flowers represent—the fact that we have a creative, loving God who feeds and clothes His people in splendor. Amen.

A DIRECT LINE TO HEAVEN

Daily reading: Matthew 19:13–15; Luke 5:16; 6:12; 11:1–13
Key passage: Jesus often withdrew to the wilderness for prayer.
(Luke 5:16)

I recently experienced one of the most frustrating and disorienting days of my life. I was an absolute bear to live with, lashing out at everyone in the house and winding up in tears at several points throughout the day. I wanted to crawl under the covers, go back to sleep, and wake up to a new day, only to discover that the one I was currently experiencing was just a bad dream.

The problem, I assure you, wasn't hormonal. It was technical. I had lost two things I could not function without: my cell phone and my laptop power cord.

I had lost my cell phone under a hotel bed in Washington, D.C., where we'd stayed a few days prior. I felt overwhelmingly out-of-touch a thousand miles away from my phone. People would come to mind throughout the day, and I would think, *Oh, I need to call him* or *Oh, I need to call her*, but then I'd realize that the person's number was stored on my cell phone. I worried about those who might be calling me and wondering why I wasn't returning their calls. I feared they might think I was trying to avoid them. All I could do was hope they would leave a message so I could get back to them eventually.

And my power cord? I had left it at another hotel during a women's retreat. I made it home with my laptop but not the power cord. Thinking I had at least two or three hours of battery power left, I was disappointed to discover that my son had drained the battery the night before, playing video pinball. I looked for my daughter's laptop but assumed she had it at school when I couldn't find it in the rubble of her room. I borrowed my husband's computer, which gave me a glimmer of hope that I could get in touch with people via e-mail. But then it froze up. "Oh, it's been doing that every once in a while. You'll have to let the four-hour battery run out before you can try to boot it up again," Greg explained.

Not only was I unable to read or send e-mails, I couldn't do any writing either. The ideas stirring in my head that day would have to wait, running the risk of growing stale or disappearing altogether if I didn't write them down on paper (does anyone do that anymore?). I couldn't even send some thank-you notes, because my entire address book was on my computer!

One of the downfalls of living in the secluded countryside is that we're at least forty-five minutes from civilization, so I couldn't pick up an extra power cord at a nearby Circuit City or CompUSA store, and Greg wasn't going into town until the next day. On the brink of emotional collapse, I declared the day a wash and questioned, *Lord, what are You trying to teach me?*

His response wouldn't have been clearer if it had been audible. *I'm here for you, Shannon. You may think you are at a productive standstill, but there's nothing more productive you could be doing than disconnecting from everything and everyone and fellowshiping with Me all day.* God knew I was in desperate need of a sabbatical, and when I chose to spend the day just reading, praying, resting, and connecting with Him, my tears of frustration evolved into tears of relief and eventually joy.

Aren't you thankful that we have a direct line to heaven? We never have to ask God, "Can You hear me now?" We don't need a cell phone to reach Him, nor do we need a wireless Internet connection. God is always open to receive us directly into His presence—no line, no waiting, no bad service. He's better than Wal-Mart, open 24/7, but never closing for major holidays. His energies far outlast the Energizer Bunny. His availability is never hindered, His attention never divided, His mind never distracted. He's forever here for you, regardless of why you are calling on Him or how long it's been since He's heard from you.

If you've not "unplugged" from life lately, do so soon and become a God-hog for a while. Take advantage of your direct line to heaven, spending all the time you need, basking in your heavenly Bridegroom's lavish love for you.

HOLDING HIS HAND

Who in my life gives me the gift of undivided time, attention, and affection any time and every time I desire it? How does it make me feel to know that my heavenly Bridegroom wants to give me such a generous gift?

_____

_____

_____

_____

How often do I utilize my direct line to heaven? How might I be inspired to connect more often if I made it a point to "unplug" from everything else on occasion?

_____

_____

_____

_____

God,

Forgive us for the many distractions we entertain each day that prevent us from spending the time in Your presence that we desperately need. Thank You for the generous gift of Your unlimited time and undivided attention. Inspire us to take advantage of our direct line to heaven more often. Amen.

FREE FINANCIAL ADVICE

Daily reading: Matthew 25:14–30; Mark 10:17–31; 12:41–44

Key passage: Jesus went over to the collection box in the Temple and sat and watched as the crowds dropped in their money. Many rich people put in large amounts. Then a poor widow came and dropped in two pennies. He called his disciples to him and said, "I assure you, this poor widow has given more than all the others have given. For they gave a tiny part of their surplus, but she, poor as she is, has given everything she has." (Mark 12:41–44)

When I was growing up, one of the most memorable moments of our weekly worship services was the passing of the offering plate. As a little girl, I had no money of my own to deposit, but Mom always fished a little something from the bottom of her purse for me to contribute. On the rare occasions when she had no loose change, she'd fold her check and place it in my hands, allowing me the privilege of offering it to God. She did all this in hopes that I would someday know the joy of giving back to God a portion of what He gives me.

Allison is another mom who wanted to shape her daughter into a wise steward. She would frequently tell three-year-old Megan about God's generosity. "God is responsible for everything in our lives," Allison explained.

"God gives us our breath, our strength, our jobs, our money, our food, and our cars, and God is the One who built this new house for us." Megan smiled, sending her mom a clear signal that she understood the message—*our God is good.*

One day while they were outside playing in their new front yard, their building contractor drove by in his truck en route to another job site. Megan asked Allison, "Mommy, who is that man who just waved at us?"

Allison explained, "That's the man who built our house."

Astonished and star-struck, Megan asked, "You mean *that's God*?"

While Megan may have gotten a little confused, her mom had the right idea. She was trying to teach her daughter lessons on gratefulness and good stewardship.

I suspect that was one of Jesus' goals as well when He told the three stories you read today. Using the examples of three servants, a poor widow, and a rich young ruler, Jesus teaches us what it means to be good stewards of what we have been given—whether much or little.

In the parable of the three servants, two of the servants were wise with the money entrusted to them. They appear to be grateful for the opportunity to act as stewards over their master's money and eagerly do what they believe is best. By investing it, they doubled the money within a short time. While the first servant may appear to have outdone the second, having earned five bags of gold over the other servant's two bags, both performed equally well—producing a 100 percent return on investment. The moral of the story? The more we are given, the more God expects in return. With great resources comes great responsibility.

And the third servant? He buried the money rather than investing it. When the master came back to settle his accounts with this servant, the man gave back only the exact amount he'd been given and no more. Perhaps he felt that turning one bag of gold into only two wouldn't be that significant of a profit, yet it would also have been a 100 percent return. Through the master's response, Jesus emphasizes that even when we have been given little, we still carry the responsibility of investing and multiplying whatever we have.

He gives a similar message when He calls the disciples' attention to the offering of a poor widow. While two pennies may not seem like an extravagant offering, this amount was all the money this widow had. She didn't give God 1 percent or 10 percent. She gave Him 100 percent. She gave God her all. She placed her trust totally in Him and gave to Him with a completely open hand.

What a shame the rich young ruler couldn't bring himself to have the same trust. Rather than opening his hand to God and following Jesus' instructions to sell everything he had and give the proceeds to the poor, the young man held on to his money and material possessions with a tight fist. Keep in mind that Jesus was not giving the young man a prescription for how to get into heaven. None of us receives eternal life by being generous to the poor. Jesus was responding to the young ruler's false assumption that he could *do something* to earn his own way into heaven. Jesus was saying, *You can't buy a ticket into heaven, buddy. Your money is no good there. You can only get into heaven by trusting in Me for your salvation. You may as well give all your money away, because eternal life is a free gift.* By saying it is easier for a camel to pass through the eye of a needle than for a rich man to enter the kingdom of God (Mark 10:25), Jesus was saying it's absolutely impossible to buy your way in. Our security must be in Christ, not our currency.

But we can use our currency to gain far more than compound interest. We can use it to further God's interests. We can use it to expand His kingdom. While human nature tells us to hoard our money or spend more on ourselves, Jesus knows this won't bring lasting happiness. In God's economy, we find the greatest sense of fulfillment when we give generously to Him and to others in need.

By telling us how to invest our money wisely, Jesus gives us the secret to gaining genuine riches—riches that will last for eternity. Regardless of whether you have been given a lot or a little to work with, it is a privilege and a wise financial move to generously give back to God. So, hold your hands open wide to Him, offering all that you have for His pleasure and glory.

HOLDING HIS HAND

What are some of the monetary blessings that God has given me?

_____

_____

_____

In what ways am I investing those blessings in order to bring even more glory to Him?

_____

_____

_____

How can I be a better steward? Are there other things I could offer Him in order to express my sincere devotion?

_____

_____

_____

Lord Jesus,

Regardless of how hard we try, we could never outgive You. Your amazing gifts are priceless. Teach us how to be good stewards of all that You've given us. Give us open hands with which to glorify You, and receive our offerings as indications of our grateful hearts. Amen.

A LIGHT LOAD

Daily reading: Psalm 55:1–23; Matthew 11:28–30
Key passage: Cast your cares on the LORD and he will sustain you; he will never let the righteous fall. (Psalm 55:22, NIV)

One of the first vacations Greg and I ever went on together was a five-day backpacking trip deep into the wilderness of New Mexico with a group of six other adults from our church. We'd be roughing it big time, so we had to carry everything we would possibly need, from tents to towels, pillows to pots and pans, fishing poles to dehydrated food. The night before we were to fly to Albuquerque, Greg came over to my apartment and checked my backpack to be sure I had saved room to carry some food and utensils. He picked it up and, seeing how heavy it already was, insisted I empty it onto the living-room floor. There he separated out at least 80 percent of my clothing and personal items and said, "Leave these here or you won't have enough room for everything else you have to pack. Otherwise, it's going to get too heavy for you to manage."

I insisted I needed at least two more sets of clothes and assured him that I would be able to carry my own backpack just fine. I had been lifting weights at the gym and walking around the block over and over, wearing my hiking boots in an attempt to break them in. I was all set for our rugged mountain adventure.

The next day we arrived at the entrance to the Pecos Wilderness, got out of the vans, and strapped our backpacks in place. The first half mile was a long descent into a valley. The second half mile was relatively level. But by the third half mile I was getting weak in the knees and ankles, and before we'd even gone two miles, I was spent. I insisted that we sit down and take a break, but I was in the minority. The majority said we needed to keep moving until we got to the five-mile point. Almost in tears, I wasn't sure I could make it. But what choice did I have? I couldn't stay and rest while the others moved on. There was no trail to follow. No way of tracing their footsteps. It was either keep up or run the risk of getting lost from the group. So I tried to keep up, until a nearby rock began calling my name. *Shannon! You're too tired! Take a load off!* I plopped down on the rock, wondering what I had gotten myself into. Less than two miles down, more than three to go, and I was sensing the vultures swarming overhead.

Suddenly, however, Greg turned around and walked toward me with a cute smile on his face. He reached out his hand, pulled me up from the rock, and began unbuckling my backpack. "I can't switch with you, Greg! Yours is bigger and heavier than mine!"

"I'm not giving you mine. I'm just taking yours," he replied.

Greg was carrying a sixty-pound pack on his back and now a fifty-pound pack in his arms. Me? I was carrying nothing but the clothes on my back, a sigh of relief on my lips, and a song of thanksgiving in my heart for my wonderful guy. About a quarter mile later, I felt I could manage my own backpack once again, and we made it to the five-mile point without much more stress or strain.

Greg's actions are a great illustration of what Jesus meant when He told His disciples, "Come to me, all of you who are weary and carry heavy burdens, and I will give you rest. Take my yoke upon you.... For my yoke fits perfectly, and the burden I give you is light" (Matthew 11:28–30). Jesus isn't saying He'll literally trade yokes with us, for He carries the burdens of the entire world on His shoulders. What He's saying is, *I'm not giving you Mine. I'm just taking yours when it gets too big for you to bear.*

What burdens have you been carrying? Relational concerns? Financial stresses? Health issues? Regardless of what's in your emotional backpack, I've got good news for you. You don't have to continue carrying your heavy load. Jesus allows us to cast all our cares and concerns onto His shoulders. He's big enough to handle all of them. We must simply be humble enough to admit that we need His strength to support us. As 1 Peter 5:6–7 admonishes, "Humble yourselves, therefore, under God's mighty hand, that he may lift you up in due time. Cast all your anxiety on him because he cares for you" (NIV).

Even now Jesus is walking toward you with a smile on His face and His arm outstretched, reaching for your hand. He wants to unbuckle your backpack of burdens, so that you can be free from anxiety. Won't you give Him your cares and concerns so that you can walk lightly, with a sigh of relief on your lips and a song of thanksgiving in your heart for your strong and compassionate heavenly Bridegroom?

HOLDING HIS HAND

What specific cares or concerns have I been trying to carry on my own?

_____

_____

_____

Am I willing to humble myself and acknowledge to the Lord that these issues are more than I can bear?

_____

_____

_____

How does it make me feel to know that Jesus is willing and able to shoulder even my biggest of burdens? Why?

_____

_____

_____

Mighty God,

You amaze us with Your supernatural strength! You alone are able to carry the world's burdens on Your shoulders, and You do so gladly. Thank You that we can cast every care and concern upon You and walk through life with a much lighter load. In Jesus' name. Amen.

AN EXTRAORDINARY TRANSFORMATION

Daily reading: John 2:1–11; Revelation 21:1–7

Key passage: Everyone brings out the choice wine first and then the cheaper wine after the guests have had too much to drink; but you have saved the best till now. (John 2:10, NIV)

*M*y name is Latham, and I'm from the village of Cana in Galilee. I've been to hundreds of weddings, since that's my dad's business. He is what's called a "master of the banquet." He's like the head waiter at wedding receptions. His primary job is to make sure there is plenty of food and drinks for all the guests and that it is being distributed fairly and efficiently. This way, the bride, groom, and all of their friends and family can be free to enjoy the party instead of worrying about such details.

Now I've seen a lot of wedding mishaps, like the time that bride's veil got a little too close to a candle flame and a large chunk of her hair went up in smoke, literally. Another time, a little boy was eating grapes at the reception and didn't realize he had dropped one until he saw the mother of the bride sprawled out on the floor.

But I have yet to see a couple run out of wine at their wedding, for such would be an absolute disgrace. You see, hospitality is a very big deal where we come from. Running out of wine would be like announcing to everyone, "I'm too poor to keep the good stuff flowing! You all need to go home now!" Such an embarrassment would never be forgotten, especially by the bride and groom. Folks around here would gossip about that family for years.

My dad says you can never depend on the headcount that the bride and groom give, nor can you assume that everyone at the feast will drink in moderation. You have to really be generous in your estimation of the amount of wine needed. My dad would lose his job, and his reputation as the best banquet master around, if he let the juice run out. So if it looks like we may be cutting it close, we use a technique for stretching the wine as far as we can until the wedding feast is over. We serve the good stuff up front, but as people get more and more of it into their systems, it gets easier and easier to please their palates. We can eventually get away with adding three parts water to one part wine, and no one complains. It wouldn't take the prize at any wine-tasting contest, but it keeps glasses full and people happy.

But I remember one time when the situation was almost too close for comfort. This lady named Mary noticed that the bride's father looked upset when my father quietly broke the news that the wine was running terribly low. I had already done everything I could to stretch it out. Soon it was going to look more like lavender water than wine.

That's when I noticed Mary go over to her son, Jesus, saying, "They have no more wine." I thought she was explaining that it was time for them to leave, but they didn't leave. Instead they got into a conversation as if there was something that could be done about the situation. Jesus said something like, "My time hasn't come." But then Mary turned to some of the hired help and said, "Do whatever he tells you."

I was in the corner with the other helpers, scratching my head. But then Jesus came over and said, "Fill the jars with water." He was talking about the six thirty-gallon stone water jars that we used to wash everyone's hands before the feast. (The only thing more important than hospitality around here is ceremonial cleansing.) Dad was nowhere to be found, so I went ahead and gave the guys the sign to do whatever Jesus said. They filled all the jars to the brim, then Jesus told them to draw some out and take it to my father. I was wondering why He thought my dad needed a drink of water, but then I noticed that it was not water at all! It was wine!

We had been slowly turning the wine into water over the past several hours, but this guy suddenly turned all this water into wine! It wasn't just your average wine, either. My dad said it was the finest wine he had ever tasted, and believe me, he's tasted plenty. He thought the bride and groom had been hiding it all along. Jesus never told him otherwise. But I saw what Jesus did, and so did His mom and the twelve men traveling with him.

Later, I heard stories about how Jesus wasn't just turning water into wine, but also sinners into saints. He traveled from town to town, transforming people's lives just like He did that water—from something ordinary to something extraordinary. I also heard that one night He poured a cup of wine for His twelve friends and told them that it was a symbol of a new covenant He was making with them—a covenant involving His own blood. The next day I saw Him dying on a cross, with blood flowing from His hands, feet, and side, almost as freely as that wine flowed at that wedding.

Afterward, John, one of Jesus' closest friends, told me that Jesus was and still is the Savior of the world. He said that Jesus' turning water into wine at that wedding was the first miraculous sign of His glory, and that the last miraculous sign of His glory will come at another wedding feast someday. He called it the "wedding feast of the Lamb," when Jesus returns as the heavenly Bridegroom and all of His believers will be taken up to heaven as His bride. John said I was invited if I was willing to ask Jesus to transform me as well. I did what John suggested, not because it was John's idea, but because I saw with my own eyes what Jesus was capable of. I have no doubt that He can change me, like that water, from something ordinary into something extraordinary.

Will I see you at that wedding feast someday? I hope so. Oh, and don't worry. I'm sure there will be plenty of wine!

HOLDING HIS HAND

Are Jesus' miracles proof of His divinity? Why or why not?

_____

_____

_____

Jesus' concern for the bride and groom's awkward wine situation seems so personal. Have I sensed that God is concerned about my personal problems? What makes me feel the way I do?

_____

_____

_____

How has Jesus already transformed my life from something ordinary into something extraordinary? What other changes might He want to make in me in the future?

_____

_____

_____

Lord Jesus,

Thank You for Your genuine concern for our personal problems. We stand in awe of Your transformation power, and we look forward to personally witnessing the final sign of Your sovereignty when You return to claim us as Your spiritual bride. Amen.

THE GIFT OF THE HOLY SPIRIT

Daily reading: John 14:15–31; Acts 2

Key passage: Peter replied, "Each of you must turn from your sins and turn to God, and be baptized in the name of Jesus Christ for the forgiveness of your sins. Then you will receive the gift of the Holy Spirit. This promise is to you and to your children, and even to the Gentiles—all who have been called by the Lord our God." (Acts 2:38–39)

I'll be back this afternoon, honey! I promise!" Those were the last words Marie remembers her father saying as he left for work early one morning in 1982. His job as a television and antenna repair man wasn't usually all that dangerous. However, on this particular day, a lightning bolt that struck the rooftop on which her father was perched kept him from fulfilling his promise to return home that day. Marie never saw him again, and every flash of lightning she's witnessed since then has been a reminder of her painful loss.

Knowing that He was going to leave His disciples and return to His Father in heaven, Jesus also made a promise. He said:

"I will ask the Father, and he *will give you another Counselor,*
who will never leave you.... No, I will not abandon you as
orphans—I will come to you. In just a little while the world will
not see me again, but you will. For I will live again, and you
will, too. (John 14:16, 18–19)

Unlike Marie's father, Jesus has proven Himself capable of fulfilling His
promise. In the second chapter of Acts, we see that everything Jesus promised
in John 14:15-31 came to fruition. Some believers are gathered in a house
when a sound like a mighty wind begins to howl from the heavens and soon
infiltrates every corner of the room with a loud roar. Flames of fire appear out
of nowhere, fueled by nothing but the winds swirling around them. These
flames come to rest upon each person, failing to burn anyone physically, but
setting everyone's heart and soul ablaze with passion and purpose. Suddenly,
many open their mouths and hear languages flowing off their tongues that
they've never spoken or studied before. The Counselor Jesus had promised is
suddenly in the house!

On Pentecost God sent His Holy Spirit, and His presence and power
were undeniable to all who witnessed this miracle. Jews from various cities
came running to see what the incredible ruckus was about and were shocked
to hear their own languages coming out of the mouths of these Galileans.

Not only did God send the Holy Spirit to dwell in those particular
believers gathered in that room, but He also sends the Holy Spirit to dwell in
us. Perhaps, like me, you have wondered what kind of blessings the Holy
Spirit brings to our lives. Let's look at a few:

- The Holy Spirit dwells inside our hearts and minds, where we have
  unlimited access to His wise counsel (John 14:17).
- He reminds us of God's truths so that we can make wise choices and
  follow God on a daily basis in all that we do and say (Luke 12:12;
  John 14:17).
- The Holy Spirit allows us to have an intimate relationship with God
  and paves every believer's way into God's presence (John 3:5–6).

- The Holy Spirit helps us in times of trouble, particularly by interceding with God on our behalf when we don't know what to pray (Romans 8:26).
- He helps us discern godly things from that which is ungodly (1 Corinthians 12:3).
- We are equipped with God's power through the Holy Spirit's presence in our lives, and this power enables us to be witnesses for God throughout the earth (Acts 1:8).

If you've read *Completely His*, you know how much I rely on the Holy Spirit's guidance to help me intimately communicate with my heavenly Bridegroom. We'd be lost without Him as a bridge to connect us to our holy God and remind us of His overwhelming love.

How grateful I am that, through the Holy Spirit, Jesus has fulfilled His promise to never leave us or forsake us. His presence within us is one constant we can count on, and we can confidently call on the Holy Spirit any time, day or night, for wisdom, guidance, and a supernatural sense of peace that passes all understanding.

HOLDING HIS HAND

Do I believe that God is always with me in the form of the Holy Spirit? If so, how does this make me feel?

_____

_____

_____

What is the purpose of the Holy Spirit's being sent down from heaven to live inside of me? Why do I need Him?

_____

_____

_____

Can I rely on His gift of peace of mind and heart as He promised me in John 14:27? Why or why not?

_____

_____

_____

Dearest God,

Thank You for sending us a wonderful Counselor to be with us day by day, moment by moment. Let us never assume you have abandoned us here on earth without the Holy Spirit to guide us. Rather, remind us to look to Him for wisdom in all that we do and say. Amen.

PERSONALIZED SPIRITUAL GIFTS

Daily reading: Romans 12:1–8; 1 Corinthians 12–14; Ephesians 4:1–16;
1 Peter 4:10–11

Key passage: God has given gifts to each of you from his great variety
of spiritual gifts. Manage them well so that God's generosity can flow
through you. Are you called to be a speaker? Then speak as though God
himself were speaking through you. Are you called to help others? Do it
with all the strength and energy that God supplies. Then God will be
given glory in everything through Jesus Christ. (1 Peter 4:10–11)

---

*A*fter having two children of my own and watching numerous
friends and family members raise their own children, I've come to
believe that God weaves something special into each person who comes into
this world. As babies blossom into children, teens, and then young adults, it's
fascinating to watch their gifts and strengths emerge and their spirits begin to
shine.

God gave each of us unique abilities when He created us. These "spiritual gifts" serve a twofold purpose. They are intended to strengthen us spiritually and to strengthen the church as a whole.

The topic of spiritual gifts is always an interesting one to hear Christians discussing. Why? Because there are no hard-and-fast rules to discerning or applying our spiritual gifts. We are each so incredibly unique in our personalities, our upbringings, our life experiences, our educations, our vocational pursuits, our natural bents, and so on. Two people can have similar gifts yet follow dissimilar paths and lead very different lifestyles.

Unfortunately, many Christians have never identified their own spiritual gifts. In fact, some believe that they don't have *any.* They are ignorant, and therefore neglectful, of the spiritual gifts God has given them. In his book *Honest to God?* Bill Hybels presents the following list of spiritual gifts mentioned in Scripture:

Classifications of Spiritual Gifts[1]

Speaking Gifts

Prophecy   Teaching

People Intensive Gifts

Counseling   Hospitality
Creative Communications   Leadership
Encouragement   Mercy
Evangelism   Shepherding

Service Gifts

Administration   Giving
Craftsmanship   Helps

Support Gifts

Apostleship   Knowledge
Discernment   Miracles
Faith   Tongues
Healing   Wisdom
Interpretation

Too bad we aren't born with labels that state "Born to Be a Teacher" or "Created for Nursing" or "God's Gift to the Business World." That would simplify matters, but then we'd miss out on the fascinating journey of discovering for ourselves what strengths and gifts God placed in each of us. If we don't get stressed over it, we can actually have great fun going through life identifying our likes and dislikes, our passions and repulsions, our gifts, our talents, and our callings.

Why do you need to recognize these things? Because your spiritual gifts are the best indicator of *why* you were created. Everyone is here on this earth for a purpose. There are no accidents, and God certainly had a divine purpose for creating you. He had something unique in mind—some special job or role that only you can play—when He knit you together. There has never been another person like you, and there will never be another one like you. You are one of a kind. You are special. You have a purpose. God has a plan for your life. You may not yet know what that plan is, but God does. Psalm 139:13–16 and Jeremiah 29:11 confirm it:

You made all the delicate, inner parts of my body
    and knit me together in my mother's womb.
Thank you for making me so wonderfully complex!
    Your workmanship is marvelous—and how well I know it.
You watched me as I was being formed in utter seclusion,
    as I was woven together in the dark of the womb.
You saw me before I was born.
    Every day of my life was recorded in your book.
Every moment was laid out
    before a single day had passed.

"For I know the plans I have for you," says the LORD. "They are plans for good and not for disaster, to give you a future and a hope."

Did you catch that? You are wonderfully and marvelously made! And God has a plan for every day of your life. A *good* plan—far better than what you could come up with on your own. What might God's plan be? Your spiritual gifts give you a glimpse into the possibilities. (See chapter 11 in the lead book, *Completely His*, for more ways to discern your spiritual gifts and passions.)

To help you grasp the basic truths of the passages you read today, the following is a list of ten principles to give a better understanding of the concept of spiritual gifts:

1. We have different gifts, and we each should be willing to use them to bless others (Romans 12:1–8).
2. We shouldn't be ignorant about our spiritual gifts (1 Corinthians 12:1).
3. There are different kinds of gifts, but all are given by God (1 Corinthians 12:4–6).
4. God determines who gets what gifts (1 Corinthians 12:8–11).
5. Each spiritual gift serves a purpose that benefits the body of Christ (1 Corinthians 12:12–20).
6. We are all interdependent upon one another's spiritual gifts (1 Corinthians 12:21–31).
7. No spiritual gift is effective if devoid of love (1 Corinthians 13).
8. We are to desire spiritual gifts not for our own benefit, but for the benefit of others (1 Corinthians 12:7; 1 Corinthians 14).
9. As each person exercises their gifts, the body of Christ should grow more unified and spiritually mature (Ephesians 4:1–16).
10. We should take our gifts very seriously and offer them freely out of love for others (1 Peter 4:10–11).

I realize ten things are a lot to remember, so let's boil them down to the one most important concept. What I want you to always keep in mind is:

Spiritual gifts are not just God's gifts to us.
They are God's gifts to the world, to be delivered through us.

If we hide our spiritual gifts beneath a blanket of insecurity and fear, we are robbing others of the gifts God intended them to have. Throw off that blanket and let your gifts shine, girlfriend! You'll not only bless the world, but you'll also feel great joy, confidence, and strength as you exercise your spiritual gifts, as she who refreshes others will herself be refreshed (Proverbs 11:25).

HOLDING HIS HAND

Of those spiritual gifts listed on page 62, which do I suspect God wove into the fibers of my being when He created me? What gives me this impression?

If I were to neglect my spiritual gifts rather than exercise them freely, who ultimately loses out? Me? God's people? God Himself? Or all of these?

If I discover and exercise my spiritual gifts, what do I suppose God might be able to do in and through me? How might He be able to bless others through my gifts and talents?

Heavenly Creator,

Thank You so much for weaving many spiritual gifts into each of us when You knit us together in our mothers' wombs. Help us to discover exactly what those gifts are, and inspire us to freely use them to bless others and bring even more glory to You! Amen.

A GREENER PASTURE

Daily reading: Psalms 23; 100; Matthew 18:12–14; Hebrews 13:20–21
Key passage: Acknowledge that the LORD is God! He made us, and we are his. We are his people, the sheep of his pasture. (Psalm 100:3)

I was recently walking and talking with a young woman (I'll call her Kelly) who had only been a Christian for one year. At thirteen, she had lost her mother to cancer, which left a hole in her heart that she had spent almost a decade trying to fill. Kelly talked about her struggles to live the "right" way and the temptation she often felt to go back to her former "party" lifestyle of medicating her emotional pain with alcohol and sex. "Sometimes I just think it would be better to go back to that greener pasture," she confided.

I responded, "It may be easier, but would it truly be better? Let's examine your paradigm and see if a shift might be in order. Of the two lifestyles, living outside of God's will versus living inside of God's will, which is truly the greener pasture? What was so green about that first pasture?"

Kelly had a hard time answering my questions.

She had told me about her lifestyle. She usually woke up with a hangover, dragged herself out of bed, popped several pain relievers, and slathered on eye makeup to hide the evidence of a late night. She found it difficult to concentrate at work and feared that she might lose her job because her boss seemed to be down on her. The highlight of her day was Happy Hour at one of the clubs she frequented. Once she got a buzz going, she could drown out her worries. All she had to do was keep the alcohol flowing and the guys coming around. She usually wound up taking a guy home because she didn't want to be alone, although most of the men didn't stay with her until morning. So she'd get up and do the same thing the next day.

Doesn't sound like a "greener pasture" to me. Does it to you?

But look at what green pastures the Lord blesses us with when we live our lives for Him. We belong to a great Shepherd, who forever tends to our every need. He loves us so fervently that He desperately searches for us whenever we stray from Him. In the Twenty-third Psalm, David paints a beautiful picture of the Lord as our Shepherd and the green pastures He provides for us...

The LORD is my shepherd; I have everything I need (verse 1). The Creator and Sustainer of the universe is looking out for me. What I need won't be found in a shot glass, a pill bottle, or a stranger's bed. All I need, God has provided.

He lets me rest in green meadows; he leads me beside peaceful streams (verse 2). He provides a place of refuge, a place for me to go where I will be protected and at peace. He satisfies my mind, heart, body, and soul with the richest of nourishment.

He renews my strength. He guides me along right paths, bringing honor to his name (verse 3). He gives me power over my every desire, so that my flesh doesn't need to rule me. His Spirit is alive and well inside of me, leading me to make choices that lead to a life of fulfillment. When I obey His leading, not only am I a stronger, happier person, but I also bring Him glory and honor, which fulfills my purpose in life.

Even when I walk through the dark valley of death, I will not be afraid, for you are close beside me. Your rod and your staff protect and comfort me (verse 4). I never have to be alone, for God is always with me, both in life and in death. I have no reason or need to fear, because I can sense His presence moment by moment and draw comfort from His constant companionship.

You prepare a feast for me in the presence of my enemies. You welcome me as a guest, anointing my head with oil. My cup overflows with blessings (verse 5). God delights in my presence as well and actively demonstrates His favor in my life so that others will know that I am His beloved and that He cares for His own. I couldn't ask to be more welcome in His presence or more cherished in His heart. God is absolutely smitten with me, and He wants the world to know it.

Surely your goodness and unfailing love will pursue me all the days of my life, and I will live in the house of the LORD forever (verse 6). God's goodness diligently chases after me. I cannot outrun His lavish love. There is no way that He will ever forsake me or forget about me. He has prepared a place for me so that I can dwell with Him in an eternal paradise, forever and ever.

Abundant provision...peaceful rest...renewed strength...vigilant protection...countless blessings...eternal security in the arms of the Lover of our souls... Who could possibly desire or even imagine a greener pasture than this?

HOLDING HIS HAND

What things do I mistake as being a "greener pasture" than a godly life? What makes them seem so appealing?

_____

_____

_____

_____

Are these other things truly better or just easier to run to when I am hurting? Why?

_____

_____

_____

_____

Is there any greener pasture on earth than the one that God has already gift-wrapped for us when He gave us the Lord as our great Shepherd? Why or why not?

_____

_____

_____

_____

Dearest Lord,

We are so blessed to have You as our great Shepherd, as You are so incredibly and immeasurably good to us. Thank You for leading us into a relationship with You where all of our physical, mental, emotional, and spiritual needs are provided for in abundance. Remind us that there is no greener pasture than an intimate, loving relationship with You.
Amen.

A RICH REWARD

Daily reading: Matthew 24:42–47; Revelation 19:6–9

Key passage: You also must be ready all the time. For the Son of Man will come when least expected.

Who is a faithful, sensible servant to whom the master can give the responsibility of managing his household and feeding his family? If the master returns and finds that the servant has done a good job, there will be a reward. (Matthew 24:44–46)

I am frequently inspired by the magnificent illustrations biblical writers often use. However, even though I know that all of Scripture is inerrant and inspired by God, I have a confession to make. I occasionally find myself questioning the writer's choice of words. For example, "Let us be glad" (Revelation 19:7) when we are ushered into the wedding feast of the Lamb? Just *glad*?

I'm not trying to knock John's literary style, but I'm *glad* when I get the kids to the bus stop on time. I'm glad when I remember to take the brownies out of the oven before they burn. I'm glad when I get eight hours of sleep without a pack of coyotes howling. If I may translate this passage using the SEV (Shannon Ethridge Version), I'd say something more along the lines of, "Let us clear the aisle for some triple back flips, for we'll be so overwhelmed with joy as we meet our heavenly Bridegroom that we'll be completely unable to contain ourselves!"

If you knew for certain Jesus was returning within the next month, how would you spend your time? Would you bother with things like weeding the flower bed, organizing your kitchen cabinets, or scheduling dentist appointments for the kids? Probably not. Chances are that if you knew you were going to see your heavenly Bridegroom soon, you'd focus on preparing for His arrival. How? By fanning the flame you carry in your heart for Him, and by focusing on the things that matter most to God—your relationships with Jesus, family, and friends—and by making sure that all of your loved ones know of Jesus' imminent return so that they can prepare themselves as well.

Knowing that she was about to be ushered into the presence of her heavenly Bridegroom, Wendy Coleman did exactly that. Wendy was the stepdaughter of Gary Jarstfer, the man whom I wrote about in the first chapter of *Completely His*. Wendy was diagnosed with ovarian cancer on March 17, 2004, and given only four months to live. Although her time here on earth was graciously extended, she finally went to be with the Lord on November 4, 2006, at the age of forty-nine, leaving behind a husband, four beautiful children, and a host of others who loved her dearly. During the weeks that hospice said would be her last, I flew to North Carolina to spend time with her and assist her family in making the proper arrangements. While I was there, I witnessed how a true bride of Christ lives her last days on earth.

Just as her life had a purpose, Wendy also wanted her death to have a purpose. Her deepest desire was that all of her family and friends would know Christ intimately and experience His power and peace. Although Wendy had been occupied with getting her house in order to make things easier on her family after her death, things that fill a typical to-do list became less and less important to her, and God and the people she loved became more important than ever.

Wendy had a steady stream of visitors to her bedside, where she spoke spiritual blessings over them. She made many calls to ask forgiveness of those she felt she had wronged in some way. She talked unashamedly of her passionate love for her Savior, frequently worshiped Him wholeheartedly with family and friends and took communion in celebration of being on the threshold of heaven. Although her body was ravaged by cancer, and the intense pain she felt was almost unbearable, her love for her Bridegroom never wavered. Through parched lips, she whispered His name over and over, "Jesus," with a sweet smile of anticipation on her face.

Wendy was faithful to God with her life, and now she was faithful in death. In fact, she was showing us by example how to die—not cursing God for her seemingly premature departure from earth, but rejoicing in the life He had blessed her with and eagerly anticipating the beautiful place He had prepared for her in heaven. In my opinion, she absolutely glowed with purpose and passion as she was leaving this earth. I can only imagine the rich rewards awaiting her in heaven when her beloved Bridegroom received her spirit. Surely He was pleased at how well she represented His love to others even in her final days. Surely she was overwhelmed by His lavish praises and exuberantly offered hers to Him as well.

God longs for all of us to have purpose, both in life and in death. He desires that we passionately love Him and show His love to others. By doing so, we are preparing for the great wedding feast of the Lamb and can anticipate all of the extravagant blessings that await Christ's spiritual bride.

Although none of us like to talk or even think about death, it's a natural part of life. We will all move from life into death, then be ushered over the threshold into eternal life if we identify ourselves with Jesus Christ. So I pray that just like Wendy, you will spend your life eagerly anticipating your heavenly Bridegroom's welcome in heaven.

HOLDING HIS HAND

If I knew I only had one month left on earth, what would my priorities be?

_____

_____

_____

What am I doing on earth that God will reward me for when I meet Him in heaven?

_____

_____

_____

What rewards can we enjoy this side of heaven simply by being prepared to go to the other side?

_____

_____

_____

Magnificent, Holy Father,

Fill our hearts with an even greater passion for You. Fan the flame we carry for You into a raging fire. Let us be all-consumed with preparing for the moment when we'll see Jesus, and help us inspire others to prepare themselves as well. Amen.

THE POWER TO PARDON

Daily reading: Matthew 6:14–15; 18:21–35

Key passage: Peter came to him and asked, "Lord, how often should I forgive someone who sins against me? Seven times?"

"No!" Jesus replied, "seventy times seven!" (Matthew 18:21–22)

---

*Y*esterday you read of how I spent a week with Wendy Coleman and her family during some of her last days on earth. It was by far the most time I'd ever had the privilege of spending with her stepfather, Gary Jarstfer. The entire family delighted in telling the story over and over again to every visitor about how Gary had adopted me as his spiritual daughter, even though I was the girl who'd been responsible for his wife's death. Indeed, the story caused mouth after mouth to drop in astonishment. Gary's loving actions toward me give undeniable evidence of how God makes His mercy and grace available to us, even in the presence of those responsible for causing us great pain.

However, during my visit I heard several disheartening stories to the contrary while watching a local news channel. In one story, a wife had been arrested for hiring a hit man upon discovering her husband's sexual affair. "He doesn't deserve to live after what he's done to me!" she exclaimed. A few minutes later, another story aired about two nations in the Middle East that were at war over matters that had taken place generations earlier. It seems the country that felt so deeply offended at one time has never been able to satisfy its thirst for vengeance, so war rages on and on, costing more and more lives every year.

But the story that most captured my attention was about a drunk driver whose car had plowed into another car at two o'clock in the morning, leaving several people injured and one little girl dead. The young man was being tried on murder charges, and the father of the girl was insisting that life in prison would never be enough punishment for the one responsible for his daughter's death. In the midst of his grief, the father declared, "I can *never* forgive him for what he has done! I want him dead!"

Of course, we sense the incredible injustices, and we are sensitive to people's pain. What woman wouldn't feel deeply wounded by her husband's infidelity? What country doesn't feel the need to protect itself against being bullied? And what man wouldn't deeply mourn the loss of his daughter, especially under such unnecessary and tragic circumstances? All of these people have a right to their pain, anger, and grief. When we lose someone or something near and dear to us, we are naturally going to feel these overwhelming emotions.

However, God gives us a way to eventually overcome these potentially destructive emotions so that they don't ruin the remainder of our lives. If we are open to receiving it, God can give us a special gift—the power to pardon those who trespass against us.

Jesus talked about that gift in today's parable. Peter asks, "How often should I forgive someone who sins against me? Seven times?" (Matthew 18:21). Rabbis often taught that a person might be forgiven of the same sin three times, but on the fourth time, there was no forgiveness.[1] Peter probably thought he impressed the Messiah with his extraordinarily merciful attitude. However, Jesus explains to Peter that there is *no limit* to the mercies we are to extend toward others. Why would Jesus want us to forgive someone over and over? Because that's what He does for us.

Exercising forgiveness doesn't mean we have to pretend nothing happened. It doesn't mean we weren't deeply hurt by the person's actions. Nor does it mean that we have to continue trusting this person after his or her character flaws become evident. Forgiveness simply means that we let go of our need for vengeance so that we can live without the negative effects of that person's sin. Forgiveness means saying, "I'm cancelling your debt. You don't owe me anything."

Think about it. What purpose does it serve to drag around a boatload of animosity toward those who trespass against us? Does it keep the sinner in a prison cell of unforgiveness? No. It does the opposite. It keeps *us* in a prison cell of unforgiveness. The anger, bitterness, and hatred we hold in our hearts harms no one but us. In fact, it can become a cancer that eats away at the joy and peace God wants us to experience.

Forgiveness is the best dose of preventative medicine possible to keep that cancer from invading and destroying our lives. Gary Jarstfer would tell you the same thing. Remaining angry at me all his life for accidentally killing his wife wouldn't have brought Marjorie back, or helped him heal from the painful loss. Yet his extravagant mercy has helped us both to heal.

Perhaps there are people who've deeply wounded you, imbedding a painful splinter in your heart. If so, the splinter needs to be removed so your heart can heal rather than allowing the wound to fester. Unwrap God's gift to you—the power to pardon another's sins, just as He has pardoned yours. Then you can experience the joy, peace, and complete freedom that God intends for you to enjoy.

HOLDING HIS HAND

Who have I been deeply wounded by? How so?

_____

_____

_____

_____

If I hold on to the offense, what will the ultimate outcome be? Will I ever be able to satisfy a desire for vengeance? What effect might my negative emotions eventually have on my physical, mental, emotional, and spiritual health?

_____

_____

_____

If I release the offense, offering the same mercy to others that God has so freely given me, what will the ultimate outcome be? How will I benefit? How will the recipient of my mercy benefit?

_____

_____

_____

Father God,

It's hard to imagine that You were so willing to erase every sin we'd ever commit, especially when You are completely sinless Yourself. Yet, in Your loving mercy, You chose to sacrifice Your beloved Son so that we could become His spotless bride. Help us, Lord, to exercise the power to pardon others, forgiving them as You have forgiven us. In Jesus' most holy and precious name. Amen.

FRIENDS WHO'LL
CARRY YOU

Daily reading: Mark 2:1–12; Luke 5:17–26

Key passage: They couldn't get to Jesus through the crowd, so they dug through the clay roof above his head. Then they lowered the sick man on his mat, right down in front of Jesus. (Mark 2:4)

---

*W*hat would the paralyzed man in today's reading have done without his four friends who were so eager to carry him to the feet of the Great Physician?

I can just imagine them loading their disabled friend onto that mat and carrying him to Jesus, motivated by the hope that He could help him walk again. Once they arrive at the house where Jesus is speaking, they realize there's no way they are going to be able to make their way through the crowd of people who are all just as eager to see Jesus perform a miracle as they are. But instead of carrying the man back home or waiting patiently in the yard for Jesus to pass by them, the four friends get a more daring idea.

Perhaps one sees the staircase beside the house, knowing it leads to the rooftop, and suggests, "We can remove the roofing tiles and dig a hole through the clay ceiling!" Did the man on the mat question their decision?

Did the owner of the house begin to protest when he realized what was happening? Did the footsteps on the rooftop cause suspicion? What did the homeowner think when clay debris began falling onto his head and daylight came pouring in through his ceiling? Or when the hole became so big that a person could pass through it horizontally?

And what about Jesus? Did He look up and laugh at the sight, delighted to see the faith of this man's friends? Or did He keep right on teaching, completely undistracted? As the man was lowered onto the floor, did it make others angry that he stole their front-row seats, or were they eager to see what Jesus would do in response to this spectacle?

While Scripture provides none of the answers to these questions, we can say this with confidence: These men didn't leave disappointed. They got what they came for. They got their miracle—not just a physical one but also a spiritual one—and their beloved friend walked away, personally carrying the mat on which he'd been carried. He was completely forgiven of sin and completely free to dance.

In many ways this man's story is my story too. While I've always been able to walk physically, I was once crippled spiritually and emotionally. As a teenage girl, I was addicted to love or at least intoxicated by any morsel of attention and affection I could coax out of a man. This addiction kept me horizontal much of the time, if you'll pardon the imagery. I couldn't find the courage to stand up and walk as a woman of sexual and emotional integrity. I didn't know how to be healed of my *dis-ease*. Later I was paralyzed by the fear of living without a man, so much so that I often kept at least one or two men "on the hook" emotionally, just in case my husband got away.

But God blessed me with some caring friends who loved me enough to carry me into the presence of the Great Physician. There was nothing in it for them except for dirty knees from the many hours spent in prayer on my behalf and the hope of having me experience wholeness in Christ. I'd like to think that the past decade has proved to these dear friends that they got what they prayed for. They received their miracle, and I now walk completely forgiven of my sin, completely free to dance, and completely His as a result.

Have there been friends in your life who have loved you enough to carry you into the presence of the Great Physician, where you could be healed of your every heartache and pain? If so, can you imagine where you'd be without them? Have you thanked them for caring enough about you to speak the truth in love to you and for lifting you up in prayer? Better yet, have you thanked the Lord for sending these friends into your life? Friends are truly gifts from God, gifts that lift us up when we are down and even help us turn our lives around. If you have girlfriends who've lifted you up or turned you around, show them how much you appreciate them. Stand up, pick up your mat, and walk as the woman of integrity that they've prayed you'd become.

HOLDING HIS HAND

Who are the friends who have cared enough to carry me into the presence of the Great Physician?

_____

_____

_____

_____

How have my God-given friends helped me grow and change in positive ways?

_____

_____

_____

_____

What are a few ways I can show them that their efforts on my behalf have not been in vain? Which one will I do this week?

_____

_____

_____

_____

Holy God,

How awesome You are to give us friends who care enough to carry us into Your presence, especially when we are too weak to come to You ourselves. Give us hearts of gratitude for such friends, and help us to become such friends to others. Amen.

HONOR FOR HUMILITY

Daily reading: Matthew 23:1–12; Luke 18:9–14; John 12:26

Key passage: Those who exalt themselves will be humbled, and those who humble themselves will be exalted. (Matthew 23:12)

Humble/Humbly/Humility. Some of the definitions found in the *Merriam-Webster Dictionary* for these words include (1) a state of not acting proudly, haughtily, or arrogantly; (2) offered in a spirit of deference or submission; (3) insignificant, unpretentious. While each of these definitions could serve us well in our pursuit of humility, the definition I often use is "a willingness to be known for who we really are—the good, the bad, and the ugly."

God deeply desires to honor the humble. Turn to *Webster's* once again, and you'll see *honor* described as having a good name or reputation, public esteem, respect, fame, recognition, privilege, credit, and exalted title or rank. Sounds pretty great, huh? Perhaps humility is a relatively small price to pay for such rich rewards after all!

The tax collector we read about today embodied the definition of humility, and God certainly awarded him with honor in return. He wasn't proud or haughty or arrogant. He offered his prayer in a spirit of deference or submission to God. He considered himself insignificant in comparison to God's significance. He wasn't pretending to be anything that he was not. He was a sinner. Plain and simple. No denying it. No hiding it. No justifying it. No arguing about it. Just pleading an honest case. In recognizing his "sinner" status, the tax collector acknowledged and exalted God's "Savior" status. He recognized that God's mercy was the only remedy for his spiritual ailments.

On the flip side, the Pharisee's prayer was full of pride and self-exaltation. He boasted, "I thank you, God, that I am not a sinner like everyone else, especially like that tax collector over there! For I never cheat, I don't sin, I don't commit adultery, I fast twice a week, and I give you a tenth of my income" (Luke 18:11–12).

In case you didn't catch it, let me rephrase this prayer to reveal what was truly in this Pharisee's heart. "Since I'm on a much higher spiritual plane than everyone else, I can rely on my own goodness in order to earn favor with You, God. In fact, I'm so great that You can save Your mercy for someone else. Don't You want me as Your 'second in charge' since I'm so perfect?" He may as well have slapped Jesus in the face or spit on the blood He shed on the cross to say, "No thanks. I don't need Your sacrifice!" The Pharisee didn't understand that pride and self-righteousness are just as sinful as cheating, adultery, or any other sin.

In 1 John 1:8, we read: "If we say we have no sin, we are only fooling ourselves and refusing to accept the truth." While I've never met anyone who was bold enough to claim that she had no sin, plenty of Christians (myself included, I confess) forget to put others above ourselves. We proudly assume that we have more favor from God than some others because of the things we do or refrain from doing. We talk of our Quiet-Time revelations as if we spend hours every day with the Lord, when it was really just a quick conversation while we were driving to work. We find ourselves in arguments with spouses, children, friends, or co-workers, proudly insisting that we are right and they are wrong. Our prideful attitude causes us to miss out on God's blessing.

However, if we consider others more important than ourselves, God will honor us. If we recognize the intrinsic good in people simply because they are children of God… if we remember that we are as capable of falling into sin as anyone else… if we accept the fact that our opinions aren't the only ones that matter… if we recognize our spiritual shortcomings and acknowledge God's long arm of mercy as our only source of hope… if we don't try to impress others by pretending to appear more holy or perfect than we really are, then we will avoid pride's snare. We will please God with our humble attitude. And we will posture ourselves to receive the honor God desires to bestow on His precious children.

HOLDING HIS HAND

Has self-righteousness or pride been a stumbling block in my spiritual life? If so, how?

_____

_____

_____

Has pride negatively affected my friendships? my marriage? my relationships with co-workers or children?

_____

_____

_____

Am I the kind of person who always has to be right or have the last word? If so, why?

_____

_____

_____

If I embraced a humble attitude, what difference would it make in my relationships with family? with friends? with co-workers? with God?

_____

_____

_____

Heavenly Father,

We acknowledge that sometimes our attitude can more resemble the Pharisee's than the tax collector's, but we thank You that You can change that in us. Give us humble hearts. Help us to think more highly of others and less highly of ourselves. In Jesus' name. Amen.

A HUGE SPIRITUAL HARVEST

Daily reading: Matthew 13:1–23; Mark 4:1–20; Luke 8:4–21
Key passage: The good soil represents the hearts of those who truly accept God's message and produce a huge harvest—thirty, sixty, or even a hundred times as much as had been planted. (Matthew 13:23)

When I rented my own little duplex in Fort Worth, Texas, I was eager to spruce it up and give it a touch of my own personality. As soon as I had a free Saturday, I drove to the local plant nursery and picked out several boxwood bushes to line the front of my porch, as well as two small watermelon-colored crape myrtles to plant at the end of my walkway. I also purchased a shovel and a water hose, thinking I was in business and ready to landscape. I headed back to the house, eager to dig in the dirt and get my decorative plants in place.

As I prepared the black soil, I noticed that it was very dry and rocky. However, I figured I could just add some water and the roots would grow through the small pebbles. After several weeks, however, I noticed that my boxwoods were looking a little brown and my crape myrtles seemed a little sad. I just kept adding water, hoping for the best. When I moved less than a year later, I'm sure the landlord felt the need to undo all my landscaping efforts before showing the house to another prospective tenant. I had tried my best, but the plants had continued to languish. I had failed miserably.

A few years later I married a man with a green thumb. We bought our first house, and within months Greg had all the neighbors talking about what an incredible yard we had. People would interrupt their evening walk just to knock on our door to ask how we got our grass so green, our impatiens to look so impressive, or our ferns so fantastic. Greg had planted a few grass plugs among some patches of dirt, and a few weeks later the lawn was a thick carpet of cool St. Augustine grass beneath our feet. Several small flats of plants with tiny buds would soon burst into a long, lush bed of colorful flowers, decorating our yard from one corner of the house to the other. Greg was carefully sowing scrawny little wannabe plants in the ground, and God was blessing his efforts by turning them into horticultural wonders!

Obviously, Greg's growing methods were far more effective than my "just dig a hole and drop it in" planting method. He spent weeks tilling the soil, fertilizing, and composting, but I had failed to see the importance of cultivating a rich, fertile soil in which the plants would easily take root and grow.

Ironically, the same thing that was happening in the front yard of my duplex was also happening in my heart during that season of my life. I had attended church growing up (mainly because my mother dragged me there and because there were some cute boys in my Sunday-school class), and all of my youth directors had told me about what I should and shouldn't do to live a godly life. Yet I was still a rebellious, promiscuous teen. There was no fertile soil in my heart for those spiritual seeds to take root, thus I couldn't enjoy a spiritual harvest.

At first, it was because the soil in my heart was hard. I didn't understand God's Word, and frankly, I wasn't curious enough to ask any questions in order to try to understand it. Once I was mature enough to gain some understanding, Satan began turning my head away from God's Word with the typical temptations that lead teenagers astray. Eventually, through painful lessons learned, I began losing my taste for forbidden fruit. I occasionally got excited about God and attended some Christian concerts and even began reading His

Word on my own. But my soil was rocky. I was so distracted by work, school, dating, and friendships that God's Word still couldn't take root.

But God, in His faithfulness, tilled that soil by creating an undeniable hunger for Him that I couldn't satisfy with anyone or anything else. He helped me prioritize my life in such a way that His words were able to take root in my heart. Now they nourish my soul on a daily basis. As a result, God is blessing my efforts and producing a plentiful harvest. He is giving me the privilege of speaking into the lives of women all over the world and teaching them how to let God's Word take root in their own hearts.

How do we know when God's Word has taken root in our hearts? It will always bear fruit. If we're not living abundantly fruitful lives, it's not the seed's fault. It's the soil's fault. The seed never changes. God and His words are the same yesterday, today, and forever (Hebrews 13:8). The soil, however, (our own heart's receptivity to God's Word) can change from day to day, affecting our ability to receive the huge spiritual harvest that God desires to give us.

So, boldly ask God to till the soil of your heart and prepare it to receive every word that He wants to speak into your life. Once His words are firmly planted, get ready for Him to bless you with an abundant harvest!

HOLDING HIS HAND

Do I believe that God will gladly sow His words into my heart and give me an abundant spiritual harvest if my "soil" is receptive to Him? Why or why not?

Were there seasons of my life when God's words were falling on my ears, but failing to take root in my heart? What might have been the reason?

If the saying is true that "One only believes the parts of the Bible that one actually does," how can I have confidence that God's words have taken root in my life?

_____

_____

_____

Precious Lord,

Sow Your Word into us, and cause it to take root deep within our hearts. Prepare us for the spiritual harvest You wish to bear through our lives, and let others see what a wonderful Master Gardener You are! We pray these things in the mighty name of Jesus. Amen.

A Secure Identity

Daily reading: Luke 12:33–34; John 1:12; 15:15; Romans 8:31–39

Key passage: The purses of heaven have no holes in them. Your treasure will be safe—no thief can steal it and no moth can destroy it. (Luke 12:33)

There are several phone calls that every consumer fears—your credit card company calling to inform you that you have exceeded your credit limit, when you know this to be impossible; the bank calling to decline your loan based on a credit rating that you wrongly assumed was in perfect shape; the collection agency calling to collect a debt that you never incurred. These calls may be an indication that someone has stolen your credit card information and is spending your money far more freely than you would. In fact, identity theft has quickly become one of our biggest personal threats as well as one of our country's greatest financial burdens.

Consider the following statistics:

- The number of U.S. adult victims reporting identity fraud in 2006 totaled 8.9 million.
- Total fraud amount in 2006 was $56.6 billion, averaging $6,383 per victim.
- Victims spend an average of 600 hours recovering from this crime, often over a period of years. Based on 600 hours times the estimated

victim wages, this equals nearly $16,000 in lost potential or realized income.[1]

- Even after the thief stops using the information, victims often continue struggling with aftereffects, such as increased insurance or credit card fees, inability to find employment, higher interest rates, and continued collection calls.
- The emotional impact on victims is likened to that felt by victims of more violent crime, including rape, violent assault, and repeated battering. Some victims feel dirty, defiled, ashamed and embarrassed, and undeserving of assistance. Others report a split with a significant other or spouse and of being unsupported by family members.
- Forty-nine percent also stated that they do not feel they know how to adequately protect themselves from this crime.[2]
- Ninety-one percent of respondents do not see the "light at the end of the tunnel" and expect a heavy increase in victimization.[3]

If you, like a few of my friends, have ever had your identity stolen, you know what a nightmare it can be trying to put the pieces of your financial life back together.

If you think about it, identity theft is only one point of vulnerability. Nothing we own is truly sacred. Everything we possess, we also stand to lose. In fact, the plot in many popular films is founded on this reality. In *Dances with Wolves* the native Indians lost their land to white settlers. In *Amistad*, the freedom that many Africans once enjoyed was suddenly stolen as they were kidnapped by slave traders. In *Schindler's List* millions of political prisoners lost their livelihood, their luxuries, and their lives in the confines of concentration camps during World War II. Even though most of us reside in a country where our land, our freedom, and our lives are protected by certain laws, we cannot naively assume that history will not repeat itself or that we are living in complete security.

We also stand to lose those things we often look to for a sense of security. For instance, the cool cars we drive will someday decorate the scrapyard, and the elaborate homes we may live in will someday be nothing more than dilapidated ruins. The high-school trophies that fill our attics, the college degrees that adorn our walls, and the performance awards that decorate our bookshelves will most likely be considered worthless once we leave this earth.

However, there is one form of security that we will absolutely, positively *never* lose—the identity that we have in God the Father and in Jesus Christ, His Son. This identity is the only one we can truly cling to as rock solid, totally secure, and forever unchangeable. God declares us the sheep of His pasture (Ezekiel 34:11–15). He considers us His intimate friends (John 15:15). We are permanently grafted into God's family as His beloved daughters (Galatians 4:4–6). He has chosen us as His spiritual bride (Hosea 2:19–20). Absolutely nothing can change the fact that we are forever identified with Jesus Christ. As Paul wrote to the Roman church, "I am convinced that nothing can ever separate us from his love. Death can't, and life can't. The angels can't, and the demons can't. Our fears for today, our worries about tomorrow, and even the powers of hell can't keep God's love away" (Romans 8:38).

Your identity as God's child, Christ's friend, and the beloved bride of our heavenly Bridegroom can never be stolen by anyone. Praise God that in this insecure world we live in, we can rest securely in our identity in Christ and look forward to the rich rewards He has awaiting us in heaven.

Holding His Hand

Who do I look to for my identity? From where do I get my self-esteem?

_____

_____

_____

Are these secure sources of identity and self-esteem, or will they eventually change and leave me wondering who I really am?

_____

_____

_____

What would it look like for a woman to be secure in her identity in Christ and to have full confidence in the treasures she is storing up in heaven? Does this describe how I live? Why or why not?

_____

_____

_____

Lord God,

Our roles, responsibilities, and relationships will change from season to season. However, You never change, nor does our identity as Your beloved bride. Thank You that we can have complete confidence in the fact that we will always be Your cherished child and Your forever friend. Giving thanks for You, Jesus. Amen.

CALM IN THE MIDST
OF STORMS

Daily reading: Matthew 8:23–27; Mark 4:35–41; Luke 8:22–25

Key passage: Jesus was sleeping at the back of the boat with his head on a cushion. Frantically they woke him up, shouting, "Teacher, don't you even care that we are going to drown?"

When he woke up, he rebuked the wind and said to the water, "Quiet down!" Suddenly the wind stopped, and there was a great calm. (Mark 4:38–39)

*I*n his book *Jesus Mean and Wild* Mark Galli tells the story of a group of Laotian refugees who attended his church in Sacramento and soon desired to become members. Wanting to make sure they understood the commitment they were about to make, Galli first led them in a study of Mark's gospel. He writes:

Despite the Laotians' lack of Christian knowledge—or maybe because of it—the Bible studies were some of the most interesting I've ever led. After we read the passage in which Jesus calms the storm, I began as I usually did with more theologically sophisticated groups: I asked them about the storms in their lives. There was a puzzled look among my Laotian friends, so I elaborated: We all have storms—problems, worries, troubles, crises—and this story teaches that Jesus can give us peace in the midst of those storms. "So what are your storms?" I asked.

Again, more puzzled silence. Finally, one of the men hesitantly asked, "Do you mean that Jesus actually calmed the wind and sea in the middle of a storm?"

I thought he was finding the story incredulous, and I didn't want to get distracted with the problem of miracles. So I replied: "Yes, but we should not get hung up on the details of the miracle. We should remember that Jesus can calm the storms in our lives."

Another stretch of awkward silence ensued until another replied, "Well, if Jesus calmed the wind and the waves, he must be a powerful man!" At this, they all nodded vigorously and chattered excitedly to one another in Lao. Except for me, the room was full of wonder. I suddenly realized that they grasped the story better than I did.[1]

Indeed, today's passage of Scripture displays Jesus' mighty power over all things, including wind, waves, and even our worries. After a long day of teaching, Jesus lays His exhausted head on a cushion and falls fast asleep in the back of the boat. The wind and waves begin to rise, yet Jesus sleeps on. Although the vessel begins to rock frantically and the waves splash a significant amount of water into the boat, Jesus sleeps on. The storm soon swells to violent proportions, and the wind and waves grow higher and higher. Yet, to the disciples' dismay, Jesus' sleep seems to grow deeper and deeper.

"Teacher, don't you even care that we are going to drown?" they ask (Mark 4:38). In response, He rebukes them for their failure to see past the surface of the situation. They were allowing their fear to overshadow their faith. After all, Jesus had invited them to go to the other side of the lake, not to perish while on it. Didn't they have confidence that they would arrive safely at their destination? Did they really think that the Lord of all creation would be swallowed up in a storm? Did they not yet realize that He had complete command over every earthly element?

It's easy for us to question the disciples' faith in this situation, but we often act the same way, don't we? Perhaps we've not been trapped in a boat out on a raging sea, but many of us find ourselves in the midst of storms in life, storms that rage *within*. The temper that explodes when our husbands don't do something exactly the way we think they should; the pity party we throw ourselves when we are feeling low about life; the anger that rages toward a boss who devalues our efforts or toward children who won't behave the way we want them to; the sense of panic over the illness or death of a loved one; the hormonal surges that turn us into "the wicked witches of the West." These internal storms toss and turn us. But I'd like to pose a question similar to the one Jesus posed to His disciples: "Why do we let these storms rob us of our faith in God?"

Remember, Jesus is Lord not only over all of God's creation but also over all of God's people. He can help us deal constructively with the negative emotions that swell up within us and threaten to create relational storms. He can give us the strength to bite our tongues when we are tempted to spew words that will hurt rather than help a situation. He can lift our heads and our spirits when we are down in the dumps about ourselves or our situations in life. He can show us how to earn the favor and respect of those we interact with on a daily basis. He can help us cope with any physical illness or loss. He can even help us manage the hormonal storms that occasionally creep up on us.

Indeed, if we ask Him in faith, God will give us a sense of calm in the midst of every storm that life can possibly create in us. Through the Holy Spirit dwelling within us, we are given the precious gift of peace that passes all understanding.

Once the Sea of Galilee became as smooth as glass, the disciples said, "Who is this man, that even the wind and waves obey him?" (Mark 4:41). Let us remember that Jesus isn't the Lord of just external wind and waves but of the internal storms as well, if we'll allow Him to be. God goes with us through every storm in life and will exercise control over all things that are submitted to Him. Let's hold firmly to this conviction. Let's receive the gift of peace that passes all understanding, especially in the midst of storms that rage within us.

HOLDING HIS HAND

What storms rage within me most often? What causes these storms?

_____

_____

_____

What is my typical response when I feel my emotional "wind and waves" rising? Is this method of response working well for me? Why or why not?

_____

_____

_____

What might I need to adjust in my life in order to receive God's gift of calm for my every storm?

_____

_____

_____

> _Heavenly Father,_
>
> _We rejoice in the fact that You control all things—the storms that rage both around us and within us. Give us Your peace that passes all understanding and an absolutely unshakable faith in Your ability to calm our hearts and minds, even on the worst of days. In Jesus' name. Amen._

ARMS WIDE OPEN

Daily reading: Luke 15:11–32
Key passage: He returned home to his father. And while he was still a long distance away, his father saw him coming. Filled with love and compassion, he ran to his son, embraced him, and kissed him. (Luke 15:20)

---

*A*lthough typically referred to as the parable of the prodigal son, this story is really about me, the *father* of the prodigal. It's amazing how differently two kids from the same gene pool can turn out. Take my two boys, for instance. The older one, Gabe, has always been a hard worker; he's not afraid to work up a sweat and get a few calluses on his hands. The younger, Michael, well, let's just say he's allergic to work. As boys, they'd go out to milk the cows. Gabe would hunker down between the udder and the bucket, and Michael would yell, "Boo!" and send the cow running. Gabe would come back to the house yelling about how I was going to have to keep Michael inside if he was going to get any milking done.

One time I sent Gabe and Michael out to the vineyards to pick grapes, and I watched them from afar. Gabe came back in less than an hour with his basket overflowing. He picked up another basket and went back to the vineyard to pick more grapes. He must have filled ten baskets that morning. I don't think Michael filled even one. What a character! He would pluck a bunch of grapes from the vine, pick several off, and begin juggling them. Then he'd catch them with his mouth rather than with his bucket. He's pretty good at that trick, but Gabe got furious with him. I had to go out and give Michael a good talking-to just to keep Gabe from strangling him.

So it didn't surprise me when Michael announced that he'd had enough of working on the farm, not that he did much work. Said he wanted his share of the inheritance early so he could go out and do his own thing. If it had been Gabe, he would have invested the money wisely and worked hard to support himself. But I knew Michael was going to squander it faster than a cow eats corn. But what is a father to do? Sometimes you have to give your kids enough rope to either hang themselves or tie a bow with it. I gave Michael his fair share, which didn't hurt nearly as badly as watching him walk away from the family farm. I was going to miss his free spirit and the laughter that he brought to our home.

When the famine struck, I knew there was no way Michael was going to be able to survive. Figuring he probably had already spent most of his money on wine and women, I worried that he'd have difficulty finding and keeping a job. No one was going to pay him to spook cows or juggle grapes as I used to. If I had known where he was staying, I'd have gone and rescued him myself, but I had no idea where to begin looking. I just hoped he'd know that he could always come home if he needed to.

While working the fields, I often caught myself looking around for Michael. Then to keep my heart from aching too terribly over his absence, I'd distract myself with the crops once again. But one day I looked out across the field and saw someone walking toward the house. I immediately knew it was Michael. My heart told me so. I grabbed the hem of my robe and ran toward my son as fast as I could. All the while I was running, I was saying to myself, *Yes! My boy's come home!* I reached him and threw my arms around him, hugging him as tightly as I could.

He began apologizing profusely, saying he wasn't worthy of being called my son. I told him he wasn't worthy to be called my son when he was spooking cows and juggling grapes, either, but he was still my boy nonetheless, and

I was proud to have him home. I asked the servants to clothe Michael in the finest robe, put sandals on his bare feet and a ring on his finger. All he wanted was to return as my slave, but I would have none of that. I had the fattened calf killed and a huge feast prepared to celebrate my son's homecoming.

As happy as I was to have Michael home, Gabe didn't share my excitement. He was disgusted that I would throw Michael a party just because he had to come crawling back home after squandering his inheritance. Gabe refused to join the celebration, so I went out to talk with him. I didn't want him to feel left out. I could understand why he thought I was playing favorites, but I wanted him to understand my point of view. Gabe and I had always been close, and everything I owned would eventually be his now that Michael had spent his share, but there was no way that I was going to let this moment pass without a party. I'd found the son I'd lost! To me it was the same as if Michael had been dead and come back to life! My son, my playful, precocious, precious son had returned to me, and I was overjoyed.

If an earthly father can feel this way about his son, imagine how your heavenly Father feels about you. Regardless of how many times you have walked away from Him, He has never stopped loving you like crazy, nor will He ever. Each time you return to Him, His loving arms are wide open, ready to receive you into His presence where you belong.

HOLDING HIS HAND

Which son in this story do I relate to the most? How so?

_____

_____

_____

Have I ever assumed God had His back turned toward me rather than arms wide open to receive me? What made me feel that way?

_____

_____

_____

What encouragement can I take from this passage about how God feels about me?

_____

_____

_____

Loving Father,

It's unfathomable that You can love us as You do, especially when we wander off in our own direction, seeking fulfillment apart from You. Forgive us when we stray. Thank You for eagerly anticipating our homecoming, and give us a heart of gladness when our brothers and sisters return home to You as well. In Jesus' name. Amen.

Seven Gifts in One

Daily reading: John 15:1–17

Key passage: Yes, I am the vine; you are the branches. Those who remain in me, and I in them, will produce much fruit. (John 15:5)

A few years ago, my best friend adopted two beautiful little girls from Russia. Upon their return to the United States, she gave me a souvenir she had purchased for our family—a group of hand-painted, hollow wooden dolls of graduating sizes that nest inside one another. My friend had given me seven precious gifts in one.

And in John 15, Jesus has done the same for us. This one passage of Scripture contains seven wonderful spiritual presents. In the last discourse He gave before His death on the cross, Jesus talked about seven extraordinary gifts that He extends to each of His children:

1. *Spiritual pruning.* Do you know what happens to a rose bush or grapevine that is allowed to grow completely wild? It eventually no longer produces flowers or fruit. The leaves create such a canopy of shade that blossoms are no longer fed by the sun. The same thing can happen in our spiritual lives. Our own flesh can begin to overshadow our spirits. But Jesus promises that His Father will prune the unproductive parts of our lives in order to keep the fruitful blossoms fed by His Son.

2. *Greater fruitfulness.* When a rose bush or grapevine is routinely pruned of all the excess, useless growth, something wonderful happens. Flowers and fruit grow with such fervency that their beauty and bounty are impossible to ignore. Again, the same thing happens in our spiritual lives. When we are pruned, we produce a much greater amount of spiritual fruit. In fact, sometimes our lives become so fruitful that it's impossible for others not to take notice and give glory to God!

3. *Constant connection.* Have you ever had to say good-bye to someone you didn't want to leave? Have you felt a longing in your soul to return to the presence of a loved one? Jesus wants us to know that we will never have to experience this heartache in our relationship with Him. He promises, "Remain in me, and I will remain in you" (verse 4). In other words, we can fellowship with Him and enjoy His presence every moment of our lives! We don't ever have to leave Him, and He will certainly never leave us.

4. *Answered prayers.* Jesus also promises, "If you stay joined to me and my words remain in you, you may ask any request you like, and it will be granted!" (verse 7). His heart of compassion longs not only to receive our requests but to answer them as well. Indeed, our God delights in granting us our hearts' desires when we remain in intimate fellowship with Him (Psalm 37:4).

5. *Joy overflowing.* Most of us have experienced a wide range of positive feelings. Contentment is one of the most basic, where nothing is particularly bothering us in the moment. Happiness is even better, where our mood is light and we feel a reason to smile at those around us. But even deeper than contentment or happiness, is joy. Joy is one of the most powerful emotions known to man or woman, stemming not from temporary circumstances, but from incredibly positive energy emanating from within our spirits. Jesus promises us not just contentment, not just happiness, and not even just joy, but joy *overflowing* (verse 11). In other words, enough joy for ourselves and plenty to go around!

6. *Intimate friendship.* Remember the pride you felt when one of your high-school classmates called you "friend" or shared a special secret with you? One of the greatest compliments one can give is to call someone a personal friend or to confide in her in a special way. Jesus gave His disciples that compliment when He said, "I no longer call you servants, because a master doesn't confide in his servants. Now you are my friends, since I have told you everything the Father told me" (verse 15). In addition, Jesus pays us the same compliment. He considers us His intimate friends. He confides in us about the role His Father has given Him as our heavenly Bridegroom, as well as the role He wants us to embrace as His spiritual bride.

7. *Divine purpose.* If you've ever led a group of people toward a particular goal or set about to accomplish something on your own, you've served a special purpose. Maybe your boss chose you for a challenging assignment, or your pastor or teacher selected you for a task or committee because of their confidence in your abilities. It feels absolutely wonderful to be "chosen," doesn't it? Jesus has chosen you as well. He wants you to aid Him in His special mission. He said to His disciples, "You didn't choose me. I chose you. I appointed you to go and produce fruit that will last" (verse 16).

Spiritual pruning, greater fruitfulness, constant connection, answered prayers, joy overflowing, intimate friendship, and divine purpose. What woman has ever received greater gifts than these? And who would love us enough to give such extravagant gifts? A heavenly Bridegroom who was, and still is, absolutely lovestruck over His beloved spiritual bride!

HOLDING HIS HAND

Are there any of these seven things in today's devotional reading that I hadn't recognized as a gift from God before? If so, which one(s)?

_____

_____

_____

Why would a holy God like ours want such an intimate friendship and constant connection with me?

Do I believe God has appointed me to go and bear fruit for His glory? If so, am I submitting to His pruning shears so that I can be as fruitful as possible?

Heavenly Father,

Help us submit to Your spiritual pruning and to live more fruitful lives for Your glory. Let us bask in our constant connection with You, and give us confidence in Your desire to answer our prayers. For the gifts of joy overflowing, intimate friendship with You, and divine purpose, we offer You our hearts filled with gratitude and awe. Amen.

A HEALING TOUCH

Daily reading: Matthew 8:1–17, 28–34; 9:1–8, 18–34

Key passage: That evening many demon-possessed people were brought to Jesus. All the spirits fled when he commanded them to leave; and he healed all the sick. This fulfilled the word of the Lord through Isaiah, who said, "He took our sicknesses and removed our diseases." (Matthew 8:16–17)

Like most men, Jesus loved to fix broken things. Unlike most men, He had extraordinary power to do just that.

In today's reading, He heals a leper and two men who are paralyzed, one of whom is the servant of a Roman officer. He also drives a fever from the body of Peter's mother-in-law, cures a woman of a twelve-year bleeding disorder, and delivers people from demon possession. He gives blind men their sight, and a mute man his voice. Jesus even raises a synagogue leader's daughter from the dead.

These miracles account for only a portion of Jesus' healings, yet they present overwhelming evidence that Jesus had eyes to see people's distress, a heart to bear their burdens, and a remedy for every ailment. Jesus was, and still is, a power-packed, wonder-working, compassionate lover of people with a healing touch like the world has never seen.

Let's be careful not to overlook who some of these people were and the social barriers they represented. During Jesus' day a leper was a social outcast. People who touched a leper defiled themselves, became "unclean," and ran the risk of infection. Yet, Jesus wasn't afraid to touch this leper. Jesus didn't fear being defiled, nor infected. He knew that instead of the leper's uncleanness rubbing off on Him, His cleanness would rub off on the leper. With one touch the disease vanished, and this man was no longer an outcast from society. The hemorrhaging woman was also an outcast. Any female was considered unclean as long as she was bleeding, so this woman had been a social outcast for twelve years. But not after one touch of Her Savior's robe.

What about the Roman officer's servant, and the synagogue leader's daughter? Notice that these two men are on opposite ends of the religious spectrum. The Roman officer was clearly a Gentile, the synagogue leader clearly a Jew. You couldn't get two men further apart on theological and philosophical scales if you tried. Yet Jesus granted both their requests, without religious prejudice. He rewarded the faith of both the Jew and the Gentile.

The accounts of demon exorcism are notable because they prove that Jesus was Lord over not just the physical realm but the spiritual realm as well. Jesus knows how to deal with any demon that dares to possess His people. Demons not only know who Jesus is, they also know how powerful He is. That's why they turn and run at even the mention of His name.

Jesus made it His business to bring both physical and spiritual health to those who placed their faith in Him. However, we cannot assume that we can simply "name and claim" our healing miracle. God is able to heal whomever He chooses, but He doesn't always choose to heal people. Ultimately, we must accept that His ways are higher than our ways.

I mention this because it has broken my heart on more than one occasion to see a person's faith in God come crumbling down when someone wasn't healed, despite many prayers for healing. Life simply doesn't happen the way *we* always want it to. My parents prayed like crazy for my eight-year-old sister to come out of her coma when she had an aneurysm. She didn't. My pastor prayed fervently for his ten-week-old baby to be brought back to life after dying of SIDS. He wasn't. I prayed up a storm that Marjorie Jarstfer would survive after I hit her bicycle with my car. But she didn't survive.

Are we to question God's goodness or existence when our hopes aren't fulfilled? Are we to assume that God withholds His healing touch because we don't have enough faith?

No, God says that we only need the faith of a mustard seed in order to move mountains and heal people (Matthew 17:20). But we also must have faith that God is in control, not us. We must believe not only in His healing touch but ultimately in His goodness, not just when life is good, but also when life is bad.

Indeed, God's ways are higher than our ways, so we must ultimately pray that His will, rather than ours, be done. God's will is sometimes to heal someone of his or her illness or injury. This is an extraordinary gift. Other times it is God's will to heal someone ultimately, ushering that person from this life into eternal life with Him. This, too, is an extraordinary gift and evidence of God's infinitely healing touch.

Let's praise God for His gift of healing, both in this life and in the next. Let's take comfort that demons tremble at His name, and let's rejoice that Jesus doesn't favor the Jew over the Gentile, or the Catholic over the charismatic. Without question, His healing touch is still just as powerful today as it was two thousand years ago.

HOLDING HIS HAND

Do I believe that Jesus loves me in spite of my physical or spiritual condition? What proof do I have for believing the way I do?

_____

_____

_____

Do I believe completely in Jesus' ability to heal me of my physical and spiritual ailments? If so, how can I demonstrate this belief?

_____

_____

_____

Do I trust that God ultimately knows what is best for me, whether that means I am healed this side of heaven or on the other side? Why or why not?

_____

_____

_____

Most Powerful Lord,

Thank You that You came with such a wonderful mission in mind—to heal the physically and spiritually ill. Show me the parts of my life that You long to change with Your healing touch, and increase my faith in Your ability to do so. Amen.

A SENSE OF CALLING

Daily reading: Matthew 26:36–68; 27:11–31

Key passage: Jesus brought them to an olive grove called Gethsemane, and he said, "Sit here while I go on ahead to pray." He took Peter and Zebedee's two sons, James and John, and he began to be filled with anguish and deep distress. He told them, "My soul is crushed with grief to the point of death. Stay here and watch with me." (Matthew 26:36–38)

---

*O*rganizational researchers have proven many times over that there are two kinds of employees: those who recognize the value of their role in an organization, and those who don't.

Those who fail to understand the worth of their contributions tend to be less productive, are unable to recognize how to improve processes, and are generally dissatisfied with their jobs. However, those who understand how vital their contributions are to the overall quality and viability of the organization are incredibly productive, feel empowered to make suggestions for improvement, and report high job satisfaction. These employees often become passionate about their jobs, and many consider their positions more of a calling than a job.

Jesus definitely falls into the latter category. He knew He had a job to do, an incredibly difficult job. But His work was so much more than a laborious, painful task. It was a vital part of the bigger picture. It was an opportunity to obey His Father and to fulfill His perfect will for the restoration of all humanity. Jesus' willingness to carry out His calling would mean the difference between our spending eternity in heaven with Him or in hell without Him. He would do anything and everything required to rescue His people from the consequences of their sin.

In today's reading, we see Jesus falling on His face in fervent prayer, crying out to His heavenly Father for strength to endure the suffering He knew lay just ahead. He suffered through the humiliation of being betrayed by one of His own and arrested in public like a common criminal. He allowed Himself to be spit upon, punched, slapped, and ridiculed. He was stripped naked, dressed as a king, and mocked relentlessly. I imagine He stood perfectly still as the crown of thorns was forced onto His brow. He did not try to escape any of the pain and cruelty of the cross.

Jesus could have put His tormentors in their place. He could have taken all of them out with one spoken word. Yet He remained silent, like a sheep led to slaughter. He was willing to be slain for the sins of humanity. Indeed, He considered His suffering a high and holy calling, the highest and holiest calling that ever existed. He was willing to die a painful death on a cross for us, so that He would never have to live a single day without us.

God has also blessed us with a calling—we are called to serve Him in some way—and like Jesus, we can find ourselves inspired and committed to our callings, even in the face of great suffering. In fact, I believe Christians are wired this way. We are made in the image of God (Genesis 1:27) and, as believers, possess the mind of Christ (1 Corinthians 2:16). Our sense of calling creates in us a deep desire to contribute our gifts and talents toward something much larger than ourselves. It drives pastors to invest countless hours researching, developing, and polishing every sermon from week to week so that their congregations will be fed solid spiritual food. It's what inspires physicians to work insane hours trying to heal as many as they can, or artists to paint all through the night to continue creating a masterpiece for all to enjoy. It's what motivates moms to spend the majority of their days (and much of their nights) rocking, feeding, changing, cradling, and comforting their beautiful babies. We want to make a positive contribution toward someone else's life. We want to be a part of something greater than ourselves. We want to fulfill our calling. It's what makes us come alive and stay alive.

Our sense of calling comes from God. Ask James and Betty Robison of Life Outreach International where their passion for feeding starving children and housing homeless families comes from. Ask Jane Struck, editor of *Today's Christian Woman* magazine, where her passion for journalism and women's ministry comes from. Ask Rick and Kay Warren of Saddleback Church where their passion for stopping the spread of HIV/AIDS in Africa comes from. They will all tell you that their calling to help other people is a gift from their passionate Creator. It gives them a sense of purpose and meaning in life.

At first glance, you may consider a special calling to be more of a burden than a blessing. However, too much comfort can actually kill us. Researchers at the University of California at Berkeley performed an experiment involving amoeba placed into an environment with the perfect temperature, constant food supply, and so on. They created an amoeba's paradise in which it could kick back, relax, and soak up the good life. But guess what? The amoeba died. Researchers deduce that all living creatures, including amoebas, require challenge in order to survive and thrive.[1]

God provides that challenge for all of us, giving us a fervent passion to live for something greater than ourselves.

HOLDING HIS HAND

What fervent passion burns within me? What cause, individuals, or groups of people am I most motivated to live for and try to help?

_____

_____

_____

Have I considered whether my willingness to sacrifice significant blocks of time and energy for this cause is actually a *gift* from God? Why or why not?

_____

_____

_____

If I felt as if I had no one or nothing outside of myself to live for, how would that affect the quality of my life?

_____

_____

_____

Dearest Lord Jesus,

Thank You for Your passion and commitment to Your calling, even to the point of dying on the cross. As a result, we are delivered not only from our sins but also from our self-absorption. Help us to emulate Your fervent passion for people by fanning the flames that burn in each of our hearts. Amen.

THE PROMISE
OF PARADISE

Daily reading: Luke 23:32–43

Key passage: The other criminal protested, "Don't you fear God even when you are dying? We deserve to die for our evil deeds, but this man hasn't done anything wrong." Then he said, "Jesus, remember me when you come into your Kingdom." And Jesus replied, "I assure you, today you will be with me in paradise." (Luke 23:40–43)

---

*T*here's something incredibly disturbing about an innocent person dying for crimes he or she never committed. It simply doesn't seem right. There's also something equally as disturbing about a guilty person being exonerated of crimes that he or she committed. Yet both of these things happened at a place called Calvary one Friday afternoon.

Jesus always associated Himself more closely with humble sinners than with pious saints. This was true not only in His life but also in His death. He allowed Himself to be crucified between two common criminals. One sarcastically scoffs in Jesus' direction, "So you're the Messiah, are you? Prove it by saving yourself—and us, too, while you're at it!" (Luke 23:39). Even in the midst of a torturous punishment that this criminal deserves, his heart remains hard and unrepentant. However, the other criminal doesn't ask Jesus to save him from the physical fate he knows he deserves. Instead, he looks to Jesus to save him from the spiritual punishment awaiting him on the other side of death's door.

This is where many of us want to pause the tape and interject our theological opinions. So this guy will never step foot into a church service? He'll never crack open his Bible or memorize a single passage of Scripture? He'll never volunteer to serve as an usher, teach a children's Sunday-school class, sing in the church choir, or direct a single nativity play? He'll never walk down the aisle in response to an altar call, put a single dime into the offering plate, or tip a communion cup to his lips? Nope. Well then, we say, he simply doesn't deserve heaven.

But guess what? Jesus says otherwise. He replies, "I assure you, today you will be with me in paradise" (verse 43). Indeed, Jesus is going to approach God, plead this criminal's case, prove that He Himself took this man's punishment, and then usher this criminal right into heaven! In case you didn't catch Jesus' drift, let me spell it out. G-R-A-C-E...M-E-R-C-Y...L-O-V-E.

Why does this scenario seem so unfathomable to some Christians? Because we've failed to understand the free gift of grace that God offers us through His Son's death on the cross. Subconsciously, we remain entrenched in the idea that somehow we need to *earn* that grace through our service, spiritual discipline, or righteous acts. However, such merit is impossible for such imperfect humans to earn.

Philip Yancey would agree. In his book *What's So Amazing About Grace?* he writes:

> The gospel is not at all what we would come up with on our own. I, for one, would expect to honor the virtuous over the profligate. I would expect to have to clean up my act before even applying for an audience with a Holy God. But Jesus told of God ignoring a fancy religious teacher and turning instead to an ordinary sinner who pleads, "God, have mercy." Throughout the Bible, in fact, God shows a marked pref-

erence for "real" people over "good" people. In Jesus' own words, "There will be more rejoicing in heaven over one sinner who repents than over ninety-nine righteous persons who do not need to repent."[1]

It's difficult to wrap our brains around the concept of grace, but it boils down to this: It simply doesn't matter how much we do for God. It only matters how much God has already done for us. The only ticket into heaven we can ever hope to have is the one that Christ already purchased for us. Indeed, He holds it in His loving hands until we ask to receive it, not because we've cleaned up our act and earned it, but because we acknowledge His willingness to grant it to us as a free gift.

Although our eternal rewards may vary greatly, ultimately all who call on the name of Jesus Christ to save them before their last breath will pass through the same pearly gates, whether they're as notable as Billy Graham or as notorious as Billy the Kid. It doesn't matter what your theological résumé reflects about you. Eternity is not about your worthiness. It's about the worthiness of Christ's sacrifice, as well as His desire to have you, His beloved bride, forever at His side.

HOLDING HIS HAND

Do I believe that God grants entrance into heaven to those who offer "deathbed" confessions? Why or why not?

_____

_____

_____

Is there anything in this world that we could do to earn our own way into paradise? Why are we sometimes tempted to try?

_____

_____

_____

In light of this free gift of salvation, how should I respond to God's grace? Receive it gladly with a thankful heart, or try and earn it from God somehow?

_____

_____

_____

Most Compassionate God,

We can't imagine that You love sinners just as much as You love saints, yet according to what we read today, we can't deny this truth. It is difficult to fathom such mercy, yet we thank You for revealing to us through Jesus' words and actions that we all receive the promise of paradise when we look to You for our salvation. Amen.

EYES TO SEE HIS GLORY

Daily reading: Luke 24:13–49

Key passage: As they sat down to eat, he took a small loaf of bread, asked God's blessing on it, broke it, then gave it to them. Suddenly, their eyes were opened, and they recognized him. (Luke 24:30–31)

---

*T*he Bible says, "Out of the overflow of the heart the mouth speaks" (Matthew 12:34, NIV). If this is so, what was going on in the hearts of those two disciples speaking to each other on their way to Emmaus?

Not realizing it was Jesus who was walking alongside them, Cleopas and his unnamed traveling companion seek to educate this stranger. They explain, "Jesus, the man from Nazareth.... He was a prophet who did wonderful miracles.... He was a mighty teacher, highly regarded by both God and all the people" (Luke 24:19). Although flattering, their list sounds painfully incomplete, like calling Mother Teresa a "sweet lady" or Abraham Lincoln, "a thoughtful guy." Hello? Hasn't anyone been paying attention? What about mentioning Jesus' real claim to fame, that He was the Son of God who came to take away the sin of the entire world (John 1:29)?

We get the impression the two men are not so convinced, as they went on to say about Jesus, "We had thought he was the Messiah who had come to rescue Israel" (Luke 24:21). Notice they didn't say "we think he is the Messiah" (present tense). They said, "We *had thought* he *was* the Messiah" (past tense), as if they no longer believed this to be true. In other words, today is a sad day in their hearts, because their messianic hopes seem to have been a little too high.

But that day wasn't the day for hope to die. No, that day was the day for their hope to take on new life! If the tomb is empty, doesn't that mean Jesus is no longer dead? If Jesus has conquered death, hasn't He conquered the sin that leads to death as well? Isn't this proof positive that He is who He says He is?

Oh, travelers of little faith! Even as Jesus reminds them of all that the Messiah would have to suffer according to the Scriptures, they don't have eyes to see the connection. They are still in the dark as to who Jesus really is, both in the flesh walking beside them and in the spirit reigning over them.

Finally, they sit down to eat a meal together at the end of a long traveling day. Rather than assuming the role of the guest and following the host's lead, Jesus takes the lead. He lifts the bread in His hands, blesses it, breaks it, and passes it to them. Perhaps they experience that strange déjà vu feeling, as they finally have their *Aha! I thought I recognized You!* moment. Maybe they had witnessed Jesus doing this exact same thing when He broke bread to feed the five thousand. Maybe they'd heard rumors about how He went through these same motions, breaking bread with His twelve disciples in the upper room. Or perhaps God was simply ready to give them a personal revelation of who His Son really is, both physically and spiritually.

Regardless of the reason, they finally get it. They finally get that Jesus isn't dead. He is alive! They had walked and talked with Him and even dined with Him that very night! Suddenly their messianic hopes don't seem so terribly unfulfilled after all, and they rush to tell the others about their personal revelation.

As they are all talking together and comparing notes, Jesus appears out of nowhere, as if to say, "Hey, guys, My ears are burning! You must be talking about Me!" He wishes them peace, which is good since they are all trembling like a vibrating bed in a cheap hotel room. Then Jesus assures them that He's not a ghost. "See My hands? Check out My feet! Here, I'll even eat some fish to show you that I'm really human. Ghosts don't eat fish, do they?"

Although Jesus had been telling them all along who He was and what He had come to do, it took a special miracle from God to remove their spiritual blindness. As Jesus reminded them of what Moses, David, and the prophets had written about Him long ago, and how He had fulfilled all of those prophecies, they finally got it too. Just like the travelers on the road to Emmaus, these followers also received eyes to see His glory.

Have you unwrapped this gift from God yet? Although many of us grew up in church and Sunday school, often we have a head knowledge of Jesus but not a heart knowledge of who He truly is. Perhaps you've seen Him as a miracle-working prophet or a mighty teacher, but have you seen Him as the one and only Son of God? Your personal, risen Savior, who longs to be in a passionate love relationship with *you*?

Ask God to remove any spiritual blindness that may be keeping you from recognizing the reality of who Jesus is, then get ready to receive eyes to see His glory. If you've already received such 20/20 vision of our Lord and Savior, do what the travelers to Emmaus did. Rush out and tell others about how Jesus has revealed Himself to you and longs to do the same for them.

HOLDING HIS HAND

Have I experienced a revelation of who Jesus Christ is and what He means to me? If so, when and how did I receive this gift?

_____

_____

_____

_____

Would I classify my knowledge of Jesus Christ as head knowledge or heart knowledge? Why do I answer the way I do?

_____

_____

_____

_____

If I believe my knowledge is heart knowledge, how does my own life serve as proof of the existence of a personal Savior? What difference should people be able to see in my life as a result of Christ's presence?

_____

_____

_____

_____

Precious Jesus,

It is easy to assume that because we know so much about You, we must also know You personally. Yet even Satan and his demons know all about You. Give us hearts to recognize that You are truly the Son of God and our risen Savior. Give us eyes to see Your matchless glory, ears to hear You beckoning us into Your presence, and words to tell the world of Your lavish love. Amen.

Abundant Provision

Daily reading: John 21:1–14

Key passage: "Bring some of the fish you've just caught," Jesus said. So Simon Peter went aboard and dragged the net to the shore. There were 153 large fish, and yet the net hadn't torn.

"Now come and have some breakfast!" Jesus said. And no one dared ask him if he really was the Lord because they were sure of it. (John 21:10–12)

*E*nvision the scene. The sun is just coming up over the horizon, and the exhausted disciples are eager to be back on land after a long night of catching nothing.

But then a man tells them to cast their nets to the right side of the boat. John immediately recognizes that it is Jesus who advises them to do so and declares to Peter, "It is the Lord!" (John 21:7). Peter puts his shirt back on, dives into the water, and swims toward shore, eager to see his dear friend who has just recently been crucified and is now resurrected from the tomb. The others drag in the net, amazed that it isn't breaking with so many fish weighing it down. Imagine their excitement over standing in the presence of the risen Savior and witnessing Him demonstrate His sovereign power over even the fish of the sea.

Don Stephens, president and founder of Mercy Ships International, doesn't have to envision this scene. He has lived it. In his book *Ships of Mercy,* he tells of a similar miracle he experienced firsthand. At a point in the ministry's history where they were in desperate need of provision, something amazingly supernatural occurred. One of their female volunteers was having a Quiet Time on the beach in Greece when suddenly several fish started jumping out of the sea. She rushed back to the bungalows, telling everyone to bring a bucket. For a ministry that was so financially strapped, this was a literal bonanza. But after a short time, these five- to twelve-inch herring (considered a delicacy in this region) stopped jumping as suddenly as they had begun. According to all accounts, this was the only place on the coastline where this phenomenon had occurred.

However, a few days later, the miracle happened a second time, in even greater proportion...

> Suddenly, my wife, Deyon appeared, exclaiming: "The fish are jumping out of the sea again!"...
>
> There they were again: fish were beaching themselves by the thousands. So, for the next several hours, we all collected as many fish as we could. We collected them in plastic bags. We collected them in tubs and buckets. We even collected them in wheelbarrows borrowed from the hotel. We used everything available. When we brought them back to the outside kitchen area around the hotel pool, we put them on a stainless steel table to clean and preserve them, putting them in groups of tens, then fifties, then hundreds. Ultimately we counted 8,301 fish—almost two tons' worth.
>
> The other people on the beach, several Greek families, who had experienced this phenomenon with us, were just as awed as we were. None of them had ever seen anything like it.[1]

Word spread quickly about this miracle, and soon a Greek television company arrived wanting to know how they had made this happen. Of course, every Mercy Ships volunteer on that beach knew they had nothing to do with it. It was all a gift from God.

And do you know what? God is still in the business of revealing His glory by granting abundant provision. He still showers us with blessings every day. Perhaps His methods aren't always sensational enough to bring television cameras flocking to the scene, but we can't deny His generosity. That roof you have over your head—whether it's a grand mansion or a garage apartment—God gets the glory for providing it for you. The paycheck you cash every other week, that bill you paid off last month, that load of groceries you brought home from Wal-Mart yesterday, those coins you found underneath your car seat that were just enough for the Starbucks latte you were craving? Consider all of these gifts from God.

Why does God grant us such abundant provision? For the same reason He does everything—so that He can fill not just our hands, but also our hearts and minds with an awareness of His sovereignty and lavish love for us. So, hold your arms out wide, girlfriend, and prepare to be showered with a multitude of His blessings every day.

HOLDING HIS HAND

In what specific ways has God provided abundantly for me?

_____

_____

_____

What are some of the little luxuries that God has given me in life that perhaps I've not yet recognized as gifts from Him?

_____

_____

_____

What do these gifts, regardless of how large or small, say about my God? What do they say about how He feels about me?

_____

_____

_____

Gracious God,

How generous You are to all of us! Not only do You give us daily provisions for our most basic needs, but You also give us a glimpse into Your heart of love for Your people. We count it a privilege, Lord, to receive anything from Your open hand, and we want to offer all that we have to bring glory to all that You are. In Jesus' name we pray. Amen.

ARE YOU READY TO TAKE THE FINAL STEP?

*I*f this is the third devotional you have read in the Loving Jesus Without Limits series, you've been diving deep into God's love letter to you for at least ninety days. I pray it has become a healthy habit by now and that your soul hungers and thirsts for Scripture and revelation as your body hungers and thirsts for food and water.

Are you ready to take the final step in having the passionate relationship with God you've dared to dream of? If so, you are ready for the fourth and last devotional in the series:

Completely Irresistible: Drawing Others to God's Extravagant Love

Over those last thirty days together, we'll learn about the characters in the Bible who had a special flair for evangelism, focusing on what we can learn from their lifestyles, words, and actions. We'll hold our Bridegroom's hand on a daily basis once again, searching our hearts for clues as to how we were uniquely created to be magnets for God and becoming more aware of how we can draw others into His loving arms.

If you've ever felt awkward about evangelism or inadequate to share your faith or testimony with others, know that it's a talent that must be practiced, just like any other talent. We can't always attract people in the same way that someone else can. That's why you need to be true to your God-given identity and simply be yourself. People will naturally be drawn by your genuine spirit and heart of love for your heavenly Bridegroom. Just think of how wonderful it will be at the wedding feast of the Lamb when you look around and see many people who wouldn't be there had they not met Jesus through your irresistible walk with Him.

So if you are ready to embrace your role as the bride of Christ and draw others toward God's extravagant love, let us meet once again in the next devotional.

A Note from Shannon

Are you looking for a unique idea for a women's retreat? An extraordinary experience for women of all ages, from all walks of life? One that will drive home the encouraging principles presented in this book?

Consider hosting a Completely His event that allows women to experience the joy of committing their "bridal love" to Jesus Christ, their heavenly Bridegroom.

Because a bride doesn't feel like a bride until she walks down the aisle wearing white, this event resembles a wedding ceremony in many ways, and yet is unlike any other—a sweet foretaste of the great wedding supper of the Lamb that is yet to come for all of us someday!

My ministry assistants and I have coordinated these events the past several years for groups as small as ten and as large as four hundred.

Participants describe the experience as "powerfully real" (Lyn, age 52), "incomparable—no wedding will ever compare to this experience until Jesus returns" (Tracy, age 20), and "life transforming" (Samantha, age 38).

Go to www.shannonethridge.com for plenty of creative ideas, DVDs, and other products, as well as downloadable forms to help you coordinate your own Completely His women's event.

NOTES

Day 5

1. Alaska Northern Lights, "Questions & Answers," www.alaskanorthern lights.com/qna.html.

Day 6

1. John Ortberg, *If You Want to Walk on Water, You've Got to Get Out of the Boat* (Grand Rapids, MI: Zondervan, 2001), 17.

Day 15

1. Taken from *Honest to God?* by The Zondervan Corporation, Bill Hybels. Copyright © 1992 by Bill Hybels. Used by permission of Zondervan.

Day 18

1. Kenneth L. Barker and John R. Kohlenberger III, *The Expositor's Bible Commentary,* Abridged Edition: New Testament (Grand Rapids, MI: Zondervan, 1994), 86.

Day 22

1. Privacy Rights Clearinghouse, "How Many Identity Theft Victims Are There? What IS the Impact on Victims?" www.privacyrights.org/ar/ idtheftsurveys.htm.
2. Identity Theft Resource Center, "Facts & Statistics," www.idtheftcenter .org/facts.shtml.
3. Privacy Rights Clearinghouse, www.privacyrights.org/ar/idtheft surveys.htm.

Day 23

1. Mark Galli, *Jesus Mean and Wild: The Unexpected Love of an Untamable God* (Grand Rapids, MI: Baker, 2006), 112. Quoted at Preaching Today.com, "Recent Converts View Biblical Miracles with Awe," www.preachingtoday.com/illustrations/article_print.html?id=38205.

Day 27

1. John Ortberg, *If You Want to Walk on Water, You've Got to Get Out of the Boat* (Grand Rapids, MI: Zondervan, 2001), 47.

Day 28

1. Philip Yancey, *What's So Amazing About Grace?* (Grand Rapids, MI: Zondervan, 1997), 54.

Day 30

1. Don Stephens, *Ships of Mercy: The Remarkable Fleet Bringing Hope to the World's Forgotten Poor* (Nashville, TN: Thomas Nelson, 2005), 41.

TOPICAL INDEX

SCRIPTURE INDEX

About the Author

SHANNON ETHRIDGE is the best-selling author of *Every Woman's Battle* and co-author of the award-winning *Every Young Woman's Battle*, both of which have remained on the best-seller list since their release and have been reprinted in eight different languages.

She's written ten other books, including *Preparing Your Daughter for Every Woman's Battle* and *Every Woman's Marriage*.

Previously a youth pastor and abstinence educator, Shannon has a master's degree in counseling and human relations from Liberty University, and she speaks regularly on the Teen Mania Ministries campus and in a variety of other church and college settings.

She lives in East Texas with her husband, Greg, and their two children, Erin and Matthew.

Visit her Web site at www.shannonethridge.com.

LOVING JESUS
WITHOUT LIMITS SERIES

$\mathcal{A}$ n inspiring
new series that reveals how
love without limits changes everything—
from best-selling author Shannon Ethridge.

Available in bookstores and from online retailers.

WATERBROOK PRESS
www.waterbrookpress.com